MW01124650

A GAME OF EXTREMES: 25 EXCEPTIONAL GOLF STORIES

ABOUT WHAT HAPPENED ON AND OFF THE COURSE

ROY LINGSTER

Copyright © 2024 Roy Lingster. All rights reserved.

The content within this book may not be reproduced, duplicated, or transmitted without direct written permission from the author or the publisher.

Under no circumstances will any blame or legal responsibility be held against the publisher, or author, for any damages, reparation, or monetary loss due to the information contained within this book, either directly or indirectly.

Legal Notice:

This book is copyright-protected. It is only for personal use. You cannot amend, distribute, sell, use, quote, or paraphrase any part of the content within this book, without the consent of the author or publisher.

Disclaimer Notice:

Please note the information contained within this document is for educational and entertainment purposes only. All effort has been expended to present accurate, up-to-date, reliable, and complete information. No warranties of any kind are declared or implied. Readers acknowledge that the author is not engaged in the rendering of legal, financial, medical, or professional advice. The content within this book has been derived from various sources. Please consult a licensed professional before attempting any techniques outlined in this book.

By reading this document, the reader agrees that under no circumstances is the author responsible for any losses, direct or indirect, that are incurred as a result of the use of the information contained within this document, including, but not limited to, errors, omissions, or inaccuracies.

CONTENTS

INTRODUCTION

> *"Golf is about how well you accept, respond to, and score with your misses much more so than it is a game of your perfect shots."*
>
> — DR. BOB ROTELLA

Does the word "golf" conjure up images of older, well-to-do players or staid, long games with predictable outcomes? If so, it's time to head to a golf course or catch a match in person! Golf is, quite simply, one of the most exciting and universally appealing games in the sporting world. The average golfer is around 45 years of age, but the sport is fast gaining ground with younger generations, and millennials will soon become its most sizeable demographic (Golf Educate 2022). Of the 25 million people who play golf in the US, around three million are juniors (Riverside Golf Bend, n.d.). Between 2019 and 2022 alone, the number of players aged six to seventeen has grown by 900,000 in the US, and participation has soared to a similar degree among women and people of color (National Golf Foundation, n.d.). One of the sport's most unique characteristics is that it is never too late to start. Between 2019 and 2022, around 300,000 players aged 50-64 gave the game a go for the first time!

All these figures reveal golf's universal appeal and its sheer playability. Sure, you may have to invest a small amount in group classes and equipment, but once you do, you've got a game (and friends) for life. Golf allows you to go at your own pace, choose from a myriad of course difficulties, and see big improvements in a matter of weeks.

For many, it's the social side of golf that makes it irresistible. The fact that it is an all-day event means that this game is as much about getting to know others as it is about learning more about yourself! In one game alone, you will learn what triggers your frustration, how to handle unforeseen obstacles, and how to overcome seemingly impossible complications—like your ball arching beautifully but falling just short of the hole or into a water hazard!

When you are a seasoned golfer, you know that your mindset can turn things around, and you can emerge victorious, even after everyone thinks you're "over"—so long as you stay strong. And the many stories in this book will prove the extent to which belief in yourself is everything when it comes to triumphing in golf!

Then there's the magic at the 19th hole—the clubhouse, where golfers unwind and continue the conversations they have maintained throughout the day of play. And boy, do they deserve to relax and unwind! Forget about golf being a slow and easy game that requires little ability. You may not need the cardio of Usain Bolt to complete an 18-hole course, but you do need to be fit enough to walk for hours and carry your golf bag. What's more, your core strength and balance must be on point if you wish to swing your clubs with aplomb. In a typical game of golf, you burn around 1,400 calories! The PGA reports, meanwhile, that the average pro golfer walks around 319 miles per season. That's the equivalent of over 12 marathons (Southern Tide, n.d.)!

Golf is also great for your physical and mental health, with research indicating it can help stave off heart attacks, strokes, Type 2 diabetes, and some cancers. What's more, it is a powerful buster against anxiety, depression, and dementia (Gregory, 2023)! The fact that you're not only moving but doing so outdoors probably contributes to its magic. Studies have shown that spending just 10 minutes in a green area is a powerful way to reduce stress and boost your mood. Imagine what walking for hours amidst carefully manicured lawns, beautiful trees, and calming water features can do to your state of mind!

Famed actor Ryan Reynolds once said he was envious of anyone who had enough time to play golf because it is meditative and conducive to good mental health. A myriad of celebrities (from Celine Dion—who has her own private golf course—to One Direction's Niall Horan) are completely hooked on the game.

Of course, golf is often anything but calm. Few other sports put your mental strength to the test quite as intensely. The distances covered by the ball are vast, and your swing can be influenced by the slightest change in your state of mind, your level of confidence on a given day, and the way you interact with your opponents.

Despite all the "what ifs," savvy golfers know that keeping your eye on the prize is everything because you cannot control many factors that can influence your game. A strong gust of wind, a challenging new golf course, and playing at a new altitude can all steer you off-course. However, you know that most of these challenges can be overcome by keeping cool, formulating your strategy, and following through.

That is precisely the reason I wrote this book. As a military instructor and author of *The Baseball Player's Guide to Hitting Like a Pro* and the *A Game of Extremes* series, I have devoted many years to uncovering exceptional stories in sporting history. I spent 25 years of my life as a baseball player and coach, and my research led me to uncover fascinating tales in other sports. I found that golf provided unique challenges and strategies for overcoming them.

Within these pages, you will find 25 true-life stories that display how exciting, challenging, and unique the sport of golf is. You will discover triumph, defeat, friendship, and fierce rivalry. You will find vital life lessons that will keep your spirits up during the toughest of games, and you will immerse yourself in a winner's mindset by seeing how golfing greats have handled pressure, maintained focus, and kept difficult emotions in check.

These stories also capture the pivotal moments in golf's colorful history. They will captivate not just golfers but anyone who loves a good real-life story, with all its triumphs and defeats. They cover unique events, iconic tournaments, and legendary players from golf's earliest days to modern times.

Many chapters delve into the camaraderie and connection that arose between players, even when they were bitter rivals. Golf can change lives, broaden mindsets, and usher in an era of diversity and inclusion; this book highlights the unique individuals who broke new ground in the game.

You will find stories that make it hard to hold back your emotions and an array of funny and unimaginable moments that will make great anecdotes to share with friends and family at your next dinner party. Or perhaps you'll share one while enjoying a drink at the 19th hole, grateful for being part of the greatest game of all time!

1

A GAME THAT'S TOO GOOD TO RESIST

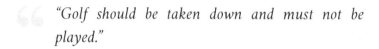

"Golf should be taken down and must not be played."

— KING JAMES II

First impressions do not always last, and this idea extends to sports as much as it does to people. When it comes to "judging a book by its cover," there is no doubt about it—golf often has a bad rap! Before enigmatic players like Tiger Woods or Jordan Spieth arrived, it was mistakenly classified as a game for old players, and the skill, fitness, and mental tenacity it required were frequently overlooked.

But these considerations were not on the mind of the monarch, King James II, when, in 1457, he decided to ban the game of golf from the realm completely. King

James II was the last Catholic monarch of England, Scotland, and Ireland; his reign is now remembered primarily for struggles over religious tolerance. His reign was marked by a fierce battle to hang onto the principles of absolutism and the divine right of kings, though in the end, he was deposed, and Parliament was established as the ruling power of England (UK Parliament, n.d.).

You would think that such matters would have kept the King too busy to worry about sports, but there was a reason why he aimed to eradicate golf, and it was a matter of national defense! In the mid-15th century, military invasions were very much a cause for concern, and ongoing wars between Scotland and England led to a need for consistent military preparation. The King was concerned that his people were not spending enough time on archery practice and too much time playing golf and soccer.

Therefore, in a now-famous Act of Parliament, he decreed (Myers, n.d.):

> *"It is ordained and the decreed that the lords and barons both spiritual and temporal should organize archery displays four times in the year. And that football and golf should be utterly condemned and stopped. And that a pair of targets should be made up at all parish churches and shooting should be practiced each Sunday... And concerning football and golf, we ordain that [those*

*found playing these games] be punished by the local
barons and, failing them, by the King's officers."*

"Utterly condemned and stopped" and "punished by the
King's officers" seems a bit harsh for a pastime! Even
soldiers need to unwind and indulge in play with their
buddies. If you thought King James II was a bit extra, take
note—he wasn't the only dramatic one in the family! His
successors, James III and James IV (both Kings of
Scotland), ordered follow-up bans in 1471 and 1491
(respectively).

Surprisingly, King James IV changed his mind when he
took up the game and became an avid player! He became
so obsessed with improving his game that he bought
costly hand-crafted clubs in Perth in 1502 and a second
set later in Edinburgh and St Andrews. These clubs are
thought to have been specially made for him by a local
bow-maker since very few craftsmen had the skills, material, and equipment to craft a set of irons fit for a king.
They were suitable for playing in open spaces like the
Inch at Perth and the links near Edinburgh and St.
Andrews. They would not have been fitting for the game
played in streets and churchyards by ordinary people
(National Library of Scotland, n.d.).

Although golf was a popular pastime, it was initially
divided into two types of play. According to Rand Jerris, a
prominent golf historian, "One was played over large
pieces of property, striking balls out in the open. The

other was actually a game that was played through the streets of a village or a town, where they were hitting a ball into a churchyard or down a street. So historians have differentiated between what they call short golf and long golf that was played in Scotland in the 1500s." (Evans, 2023).

King James IV was freed to pursue his passion by the Treaty of Glasgow—also known as the Treaty of Perpetual Peace—which was signed with Henry VII of England in 1502. In 1547, a spectacular golf course was built at St Andrews, which many consider the first-ever historical, modern golf course.

Despite the vast popularity of golf in the 16th and 17th centuries, it wasn't until 1744 that the Honorable Company of Edinburgh Golfers compiled and wrote down the rules of the game (the *Thirteen Articles*) for use during their tournament at the Leith Links in Edinburgh.

These rules were utilized over the next century by over 30 golfers' clubs. However, the Royal and Ancient Golf Club of St. Andrews created the first standardized set of rules in 1899. During this time, the United States Golf Association (in New York City) also created its own code. These converged significantly with those of their counterparts, and these two entities quickly became the top governing bodies in the game. Before the establishment of these codes, rules differed from course to course, and the community of players resisted one set of rules.

Interestingly, Scotland has a unique importance in the history of golf. The first visual representation of a game is a painting of St. Andrews, dating back to the first half of the 18th century. The Old Course at St Andrews is the ultimate "links" course, meaning it is located on sandy coast land and follows the natural forms of the land. According to Jerris, every single golf course in the modern world has been influenced in its design by the landforms that naturally occur at St Andrews. Some of the most famed American golf courses—including Oakmont and Winged Foot—recreate the Scottish landscape on American soil. Not bad for a country that once sought to eradicate golf from the map!

2

THE MIRACULOUS PUTT

"I don't know if I'll ever do it again or not, but frankly, I don't care!"

— JACK NICKLAUS AT THE 1986 MASTERS

The protagonist of this story is none other than the "GOAT" himself—Jack Nicklaus. Nicklaus, known as "The Golden Bear," won 117 professional tournaments in his career and 18 major championships (three more than runner-up Tiger Woods). Many fans would say that what made Nicklaus so great was not just his impressive number of wins but also his fighting spirit and ability to keep his mind on the game, even when luck wasn't on his side. Nicklaus, who shone between the early 1960s and mid-1980s, saved his energy for the Major Championships, choosing PGA Tour events wisely. Throughout his career, he was praised as much for his camaraderie as for his sheer ability. In 1974, Nicklaus was inducted into the World Golf Hall of Fame, and in 2005, he was awarded the Presidential Medal of Freedom.

Nicklaus excelled at golf since his earliest years, having won an impressive 27 events in his native Ohio between the ages of 10 and 17. As a university student, he took home two US Amateurs and an NCAA Championship, becoming the first-ever golfer to win both these titles in the same year. In 1961, he went pro, and just a year later, he won his first US Open (at the age of 22), beating the legendary Arnold Palmer. He bagged numerous victories in the 1960s and 1970s but experienced a slump between 1968 and 1970. It was in 1970 that his star began to rise once again when he defeated Doug Sanders at the 1970 US Open. In 1980, he won his fourth US Open and his fifth PGA Championship.

His career had been no less than stellar, but by the time the 1986 Masters came along, he wasn't considered a top threat to other players anymore. It had been six years since his last major championship. What's more, in seven tournaments that year, he missed the cut three times and withdrew from a fourth. Not to mention, he was twice as old as when he won his first Masters in 1963!

Nicklaus himself estimated that there were 11 competitors at the 1986 event that he had never met! He openly admits that he didn't expect too much of himself and hadn't prepared very well for that week. When he arrived at the Augusta National grounds, he told press members, "I'm looking for that guy I used to know on the golf course."

As cool, calm, and collected as Nicklaus was, one thing made his blood simmer. It was a news article written by renowned AJC golf writer Tom McCollister, which stated: "Nicklaus is gone, done. He just doesn't have the game anymore. It's rusted from lack of use. He's 46, and nobody that old wins the Masters" (Stinson 2016).

McCollister was famed for his objectiveness, and many others shared his perspective—since Nicklaus hadn't been a force to reckon with in years. What's more, on the final day of play, Sunday the 13th of April, the Golden Bear's performance left much to be desired. He had made the cut on Friday at 1-0ver 143 and was tied for 17th on Saturday. On the number 1 tee on Sunday, he stood at 4 behind the leaders. He missed two 4-foot birdie putts within the first eight holes and was still four back. Behind him on number 8, Both Tom Kite and Seve Ballesteros had scored back-to-back eagles.

On the 9th hole, Jack's 24-year-old son Jackie, who was caddying for his father, suggested a putting line to the left edge of the cup. Jack plated it to the tip of the cup, and the ball went right in, scoring him a birdie. "That got me started," he said, "I got loose with that because we had fun with it." He then hit a 30-foot birdie put, putting three shots behind the leader. Jackie says that was the longest putt his father had made all week. It pumped him up, and he continued to shine, achieving a third birdie on 11. As he walked to the tee at 12, he was only two shots behind the leaders.

At this point, the crowd was on Nicklaus' side. Jackie recalled the excitement of the moment: "At 12 tee, the crowd is standing up, people have their arms up, and they're screaming. It was terrific. It's probably the first time I noticed Dad getting emotional. Basically from that point on every time he approached a green or tee, you see him getting emotional, teary-eyed, having to push back his emotions" (Boyette 2016).

At the par-3 12th tee, Jack's shot went way left, and his chip left him seven feet away with a big spike mark directly in his line. He didn't make the putt and bogeyed instead. What others may have classified as a disappointment only strengthened his determination. He later told the press that this defining moment led him to try even harder on the next few holes.

He hit a drive on 13 and pulled it slightly, and it went over the edge of the trees, but it managed to hit the fairway. Jackie told his father, "Dad, that's not good on a 24-year-old heart." Jack started laughing. "He thought that was pretty funny," Jackie says. Nicklaus was 210 yards to the hole and landed the ball about 45 feet away, with the hole uphill. The ball was a little short. He landed a birdie. He then scored a par at the 14th, an eagle at the

15th, a birdie at the 16th, a tricky birdie at the 17th, and a par at the 18th. His performance on the 16th hole scored a KO over Ballesteros, who dropped his approach shot into the pond and took a bogey that completely demoralized him.

The most amazing shot of the day came at the 17th, when Jack sunk a difficult 11-footer for his final birdie at the 17th green. By then he was 1 ahead of Ballesteros and Kite and 2 ahead of Greg Norman. He aced the 10-foot birdie putt and played a masterful final hole. He was over-whelmed with emotion, admitting he had to hold back his tears several times in the closing holes.

The final wait was quick and relatively stress-free for Nicklaus. Ballesteros three-putted no. 17, finishing 2 shots behind Nicklaus. Kite needed a birdie on 18 to stand a winning chance, but missed a 12-footer. Norman birdied no. 17 and could have caught up with Nicklaus with a closing birdie, but his shot flew to the right, and he failed to save par, losing his chance for victory.

Jack Nicklaus became the first player in history to defend a Masters title, and he was the oldest to ever win a major. His competitors took their hats to him, with Kite saying, "I didn't lose this tournament. Jack won it."

"And whatever happened to McCollister?" you may ask. Jack had his sweet "revenge" when, during the post-match interview, the journalist walked into the press area, going up the main aisle to find a seat. Jack spotted him, smiling at him and saying, "Hi, Tom. Thanks." McCollister was quick on the mark, responding, "Glad I could help."

For many, the 1986 Masters was one of the best golf stories of all time; above all because it featured such a legendary athlete and human being. Jack Nicklaus inspired not only the crowd that witnessed his impressive skills that day, but people all over the world, young and old, letting them know that it is never too late to go for your dreams. He told the press, "I'm not as good as I was 10 or 15 years ago. I don't play as much competitive golf as I used to, but there are still some weeks when I'm as good as I ever was."

Nicklaus was also known for his generosity, and for the close relationships he built with other players. He has stated that one of the most useful pieces of advice he ever received was at the hands of another golfing icon, Chi Chi Rodriguez, who told him to "Take the hands out of the swing, firm up the left side, and move more aggressively through the ball."

For those who knew and loved him, what truly made Jack shine was his sheer love of the game. Speaking of the legendary Masters, his playing partner, Sandy Lyle, noted that the last six holes saw a cool, calm Nicklaus who never let his nerves get the better of him. "It's like he was playing a practice round on a Sunday afternoon. I think that's the thing I took away: There's no need to get excited." (Nelson 2021).

3

DUEL IN THE SUN

> *"Long before I ever dreamed of winning things, I played in the rain and the wind and the snow. I didn't do it for money, fame, trophies, not even the love of the game, I did it because I just loved rolling the ball up to the flag. And then I thought, that's just what British golf is, the same thing I grew up with, it's just rolling the ball up to the flag."*
>
> — TOM WATSON

If the star of our last story—Jack Nicklaus—fascinated you, and you were left wanting more of the Golden Bear, then you'll enjoy this tale, which highlights one of the most emotion-packed duels in golfing history. This one co-stars Tom Watson—the number one golfer in the world from the years 1968 to 1977, according to the McCormack World Golf Rankings.

Watson, who was born in Kansas City, Missouri, is one of the most enduring professional golfers of all time. Known for his aggressive, fast-paced style, he won the PGA tour 39 times and, at the age of 69, came within inches of winning his sixth British Open. Had he won, he would have been the oldest man (by 11 years) to win a major title (Tom Watson, n.d.). Watson is also known for his ability to achieve the impossible in the crucible of moments—those that shape and define history. One of them occurred at The Open in Turnberry in 1977, when the weekend began with Watson and Nicklaus in a tie. The final day saw the two players finish at 11 and 10 shots ahead of the field, but who took home the prize?

This wasn't the first time that The Golden Bear and Huck (Watson, thus named for his boyish innocence) had gone toe to toe. They had fought it out that same year at the US Masters, with Nicklaus prevailing (Bisset 2023). However, that match was totally overshadowed by the adrenalin-charged battle at Turnberry.

Prior to this defining weekend, Watson had been under scrutiny because of his disappointing finishes, which led critics to believe that he might have some issues as a choker (a golfer whose performance suddenly deteriorates at a critical point in performance or competition). What's more, he was coming up against a 14-time major winner in Nicklaus, who was 10 years his senior.

At Turnberry, Watson and Nicklaus were yet to prove themselves to be a threat at the halfway stage, since they were part of a crowded chasing pack and a shot behind the sole leader, Roger Maltbie at -3 on Thursday afternoon. Nicklaus and Watson went toe-to-toe on Friday, shooting five-under to score a three-shot advantage over their closes rival, Ben Crenshaw—who in turn was three ahead of the next-nearest rival.

As play commenced on Saturday, Nicklaus and Watson had identical scorecards and they dueled throughout the day until the 18th hole. The visuals were spectacular, as were the challenges. The Turnberry course, famed for its lush greenness, was dry and yellowed by the harsh sun, with rambling tumbleweeds threatening to wield their influence on the leading duo's performance.

Nicklaus asserted himself early, achieving a birdie on the 2nd and 4th, while Watson dropped a shot and trailed by 3. But Huck made his comeback in 5, 7, and 8, ending up just 1 behind Nicklaus. The competition heated up further on the back nine, with Nicklaus making the crowd roar with a 22-foot putt for birdie on the 12th. Watson proved he had nerves of steel with two birdies on the 13th and 15th, the latter an amazing 18-meter putt from off the green that touched the flag and sank into the hole.

The crowd ran frenetically between the two players, keen to catch their every move. The duo now had three holes left until victory and once again, they were tied. Such was the crowd's excitement that Watson subsequently described it as "out of control." Meanwhile, Nicklaus' caddie, Angelo Argea, stated, "I feared for my man." He was sure that Nicklaus would be trampled! Rober Maltbie, who finished 21 shots behind, recalls, "It was certainly not the genteel, well-behaved galleries you always heard about at the Open." (Lewis 2017).

As they marched onto the 16th tee, Watson looked at his rival and uttered the now-famous words: "This is what it's all about, isn't it?" "You bet it is," replied Nicklaus. The tension continued for another 40 minutes, until, with one hole to go, Nicklaus missed the chance for a birdie and, for the first time that day, Watson edged ahead (Lewis 2017).

On the 18th, a par-4 of 388 meters, Watson hit the fairway with his one-iron drive. Nicklaus was forced to take a risk, but his drive detoured to the right and the ball landed in a difficult area of rough. Watson's second shot landed 60 cm from the pin. It seemed like Watson would be the victor, but Nicklaus wasn't going to make it easy, hitting an incredible eight-iron to an excellent spot on the green, just 11 meters from the hole. He then dropped the ball into the hole, ending with a round of 66 and not a single bogey.

The pressure was now on Watson. In order to win, he had to land his seventh birdie of the day. He was just one meter away from victory. Watson recalls that the crowd was so excited that Nicklaus had to intervene. He said, "Jack raised his arms to calm people down." Silence prevailed and Watson made a practice swing, before sinking his putt for victory and achieving an astounding final round of 65. It was at this moment that Nicklaus put his arm around his rival's shoulder and, as both players walked to the scorer's hut to hand in their cards, Nicklaus remarked, "I gave you my best shot, but it wasn't good enough."

Finishing third was Hubert Green (1977's US Open champion), who scored 11 strokes behind the victor. The following year, Nicklaus scored his third British Open Victory. Watson won another five majors, while Nicklaus upped his tally to 18, with the last being at Augusta in 1986. When it came to the British Open, however, Watson reigned supreme, tallying five compared to Nicklaus' three wins.

In golfing historiography, the Duel in the Sun is considered to be the finest game played in the latter half of the 20th century. Hubert Green, the third-placer, famously remarked, "I won this golf tournament. I don't know what game those other two guys were playing."

4

BEN HOGAN: GOLF'S GREATEST COMEBACK

 "I'm glad I brought this course, this monster, to its knees."

— BEN HOGAN

In 1949, Ben Hogan was one of the most prominent golfers on the scene. Between the years of 1940 to 1948, he had secured four victories yearly, except for the time he spent during World War II as a US Army Air Forces pilot (from 193 to 1945). It was a long climb for Ben, who didn't have it as easy as other golfers of his generation.

Ben had an undoubtedly difficult childhood. One evening, in 1922 (when he was just nine) his father, Chester (a blacksmith from Texas) became embroiled in an argument with Ben's mother. Chester took a .38 revolver from his bag and shot himself in the heart, and—according to some sources—Ben was in the room when it happened. Chester's death not only caused his family great anguish, but also plunged them into poverty. Ben and his brother quickly began working to help feed their family (Barton 2019).

As a boy, Ben sold newspapers until, one day, he found out that he could make a much better living by carrying golfers' bags. At the age of 11, he hiked seven miles to the Glen Garden Country Club, unknowingly forging what would become the career of a lifetime as a pro golfer. Interestingly, another caddie at the same club was Byron Nelson—another of golf's all-time greats, having taken home 54 victories—including two Masters (1937 and 1942) and two PGA Championships (1940 and 1945)!

Despite having spent so much time on golf courses since an early age, Ben was considered a late bloomer. By the time he won his first tournament, Nelson and another player of his generation—Sam Snead—had won over ten tournaments. Ben had turned pro at the age of 17, a year ahead of Snead and two of Nelson.

Perhaps the fact that he was completely self-taught had something to do with it. He initially developed a loopy swing that was designed to do one thing: hit draws for maximum distance. He wanted to outdrive older caddies, so he would have the right to be a caddy himself. However, he was able to perfect his swing to produce such a high level of accuracy that many believed he had discovered the secret of the perfect golf swing.

These early years were tough. Ben and his wife, Valerie, struggled financially. Thankfully, Valerie was his biggest cheerleader and he encouraged him to stick to his resolve. He kept at it, and once he clinched his first triumph, the floodgates burst open. In 1948, he was one of the most dominant players on the US pro scene. That year, he scored ten tournament victories, including the USPGA Championship and the US Open.

The year 1949 also started well. He secured the win at the Bing Crosby Pro-Am and the Long Beach Open, beating Jimmy Demaret by two strokes in a playoff. The following week, he played a great game at the Phoenix Open, narrowingly missing out on the victory to Demaret after an arduous 18-hole playoff (Bisset 2023). The playoff resulted in Hogan driving back home to Fort Worth a day late—a twist of fate that led to a serious accent that almost ruined his career.

Ben and Valerie were traveling in their Cadillac along the Van Horn to Kent route, when an impatient bus driver crashed into them after attempting to pass a truck on a narrow road. Ben threw himself across the seat to protect his wife when he saw that the collision was unavailable. This instinct probably saved his own life as well! The steering wheel (which Ben had been holding) had been driven back in the seat and the engine was hurled onto the front seat as a result of the impact. Ben broke his pelvis, rib, collarbone, and left ankle. The doctors wondered if he would ever walk again, and many wondered if he would ever play golf again.

Yet within a few months, Ben was putting again, and the following year (1950), he emerged victorious at the US Open. He was in so much pain that he told his wife he thought he wouldn't finish. However, his passion for his sport prevailed and victory was secured. He had gone from a near-death experience to achieving a national championship in just 16 months! Without a doubt, it was one of the most remarkable achievements not only in golf, but in the world of sports.

Ben Hogan was an icon (Immelman 2020). He was a tenacious perfectionist who spoke few words but left the golfing world with gems like his book, *Ben Hogan's Five Lessons: The Modern Fundamentals of Golf*—a timeless classic that features the building blocks of excelling at golf, according to Ben. His words were carefully thought-out, incisive, and filled with wisdom.

He was clean-shaven, neatly dressed, and known for his stoicism and unfailing honesty. He never relied on gimmicks to get ahead, emphasizing the need for hard work and consistency. The ups and downs in his life had shown him that you can be on top of the world one day and struggling to survive the next. Many would say that his tough childhood forged a steely mind and a warrior's heart.

Interestingly, Jack Nicklaus once said that he got on with Hogan because the latter wasn't effusive. Indeed, he was somewhat of a loner. Despite his material success, he supposedly built a house with only one bedroom to avoid having to host overnight guests (Barton 2019). Meanwhile, Byron Nelson famously told Ben's biographer, James Dodson, "Ben was a great mystery to a lot of people, maybe even to himself. For some reason, I don't know why, he wanted it that way. He wouldn't let people in."

Ben's injuries made prolonged walking difficult for the rest of his life and they undoubtedly affected his game. After his accident, he won six more majors, and in 1953, he was victorious in five of the six tournaments he competed in (including the British and US Opens, and the Masters). Until Tiger Woods, no other player would win three Grand Slam competitions in one season. In fact, it is often assumed that Ben would have won the PGA Championship as well, had he been able to play in it. Sadly, it overlapped with the British Open! What's more, Ben wasn't a big fan of the tournament, as it required players to complete 36 holes on some days. His injuries made it impossible for him to go longer than 18 holes (Bonesteel 2021).

Ben Hogan was more than an example of what immense skill can achieve. He was said to have "invented practice," because he spent more time practicing than any other golfer in his time (Top End Sports, n.d.). For Bleach Report's Mike Lynch (2013) he was, quite simply, the greatest golfer of all time, having overcome a traumatic early life, taught himself everything he knew, and made the greatest comeback in history.

5

STRUCK BY LIGHTNING

"You can't teach passion. You can teach everything else."

— LEE TREVINO

Golf is a fantastic source of stress relief for people across the globe, but sometimes, it is far from peaceful! In fact, like any sport that involves being in the Great Outdoors, it has its share of surprises, many of which are caused by nature. Of course, bird watching and the beauty of the landscape weren't on Lee Trevino's mind when he woke up on the morning of June 28, 1975. He had his mind set on the challenging day that lay ahead—for he was competing in the Western Open at the Butler National Golf Club in Oakbrook, Illinois.

Lee was on a high, for he had worked hard to get where he was. He was born in Texas and achieved what seemed like "overnight success" when he joined the GA Tour in 1967 and became recognized as one of the top golfers of his time. Lee worked as an odd job man and assistant pro at golf courses close to his home in Texas, but in 1967, he came in fifth in the US Open. He was victorious at the Open in 1968 and secured the victory in two British Opens (1971 and 1972). By 1970, his earnings were higher than that of any other golfer and in 1971, he became the first golfer to claim victory and the British, Canadian, and US opens in a single year.

But his fortune took a turn that fateful day in 1975. While standing near the 13th hole, Lee and two other players (Jerry Heard and Bobby Nichols) were struck by lightning. Lee says that at this moment, his life literally flashed before his eyes (Long, n.d.). He had just marked his ball a few feet from the pin, and he was walking toward a lake. Despite the poor weather, he was confident that the skies would quickly clear and decided to keep playing. His recollection of the moment is eerie: "It was a very, very quiet sensation. I couldn't hear a thing. There was a whining noise in my ears. I know it (lightning) had me when I started shaking. Then it started stretching out and picked me up off the ground. I couldn't breathe, and I remember gasping for air. Everything looked orange to me." He discovered later that the electricity had stopped his heart. When he came to, his body ached terribly.

The effects were as serious as you might imagine! Lee went through two back operations to repair a ruptured disk that had been damaged by the lightning bolt. Jerry Heard underwent the same operation, but was never able to play professionally again, while Bobby Nichols managed to make a full recovery.

Lee recalled that his doctor found it hard to believe the golfer was still alive, since most people who had been struck by lightning so intensely had lost their lives. It was the strength of Lee's heart, said his doctor, that kept him alive. Things were never as easy for Lee after the accident. He says he had to learn to play again from scratch, since he became unable to use the same movement he had in the past. His injuries forced him to come out of the swing quicker and draw the ball more.

As El Paso Times writer Trish Long notes, Lee was almost struck by lightning a second time! He withdrew from one US Open because he was experiencing pain, and Bobby Wadkins competed instead. One member of Wadkins' threesome was struck by lightning, as were several fans cheering the players on!

The lightning attack experienced by the three players resulted in the PGA honing its techniques for monitoring nearby storms. A machine is used, for instance, to determine lighting up to 100 miles in distance.

Lee has admitted that the sight of lightning now scares him more than it did before the accident. However, he has jokingly said, "I've been hit by lightning and been in the Marine Corps for four years. I've traveled the world and been about everywhere you can imagine. There's not anything I'm scared of except my wife."

Lee was victorious on the tour eight more times, showing the depth of his commitment to (and love for) the sport. Lee won a total of 29 PGA tours and six major championships in his colorful career and even today, at the age of 84, he is quite a character.

In 2022, Lee met up with renowned golf analyst, Gary Koch, who asked him why he still played golf daily. His answer was testimony to how hard he worked to achieve success: "Well, I tell you what, this game of golf, I never had a choice, as you well know. When I was a young man with my educational background, this was the only thing that I could do and do well. And the good lord gave me a tremendous amount of talent, and I don't want to disappoint Him when I see Him..." (Piastowski, 2022).

He also told Koch that he still loves golf with a passion. It makes sense. Golf, in many ways, saved Lee from a tough life. He came from an extremely poor family and worked as a cotton picker at the tender age of five. By the time he was 14, he had left the educational system and was working as a caddy to make ends meet. He was a keen observer of the game and, like Ben Hogan, was totally self-taught.

He admits that in his youth, discipline wasn't his forte. However, entering the Marine Corps at the age of 17 transformed him completely, honing values like discipline, commitment, and hard work. By the age of 23, he was already a force to be reckoned with and soon, he was competing against the cream of the crop—including players like Jack Nicklaus.

Lee was known for his dedication to his craft, but also for always being able to find humor in even the toughest of situations. Soon after he recovered from his accident, a reporter asked him if he would do anything in the future to avoid being struck by lightning again (Kulkarni, 2021). His answer is now one of golf's most famous quotes: "I would hold up a 1-iron. Not even God can hit a 1-iron."

6

PLAYING THROUGH BULLETS

"Shrapnel and/or bomb splinters on the fairways, or in bunkers within a club's length of a ball, may be moved without penalty, and no penalty shall be incurred if a ball is thereby caused to move accidentally."

— THE RICHMOND GOLF CLUB

If you ever need proof of exactly how addictive and exciting golf is, you'll find exactly what you're after at the Richmond Golf Club (from Surrey, England). In 1940, while the Battle of Britain raged in the skies and brave RAF pilots faced the Luftwaffe in the war against Hitler, one group of men refused to let go of two things that kept many of them sane in tough times—golf, and a sense of humor! They were keen to show the Germans that their spirit of unity and perseverance could not be wiped out. Nor could their tenacity and resilience. The British government, which recognized the vitality of maintaining public morale, would undoubtedly have applauded the bravado of the golfers, whose actions encouraged others to stay strong and carry on with their daily lives—despite the devastating bombings that began on a fateful September 7, 1940.

There was only one problem for the eccentric, golf-crazy members of this club—play was a hazard in itself, since over 1,000 bombs were dropped on Richmond between October 1940 and June 1941 (Joseph 2018). Capturing the spirit of the Blitz, the players put together a series of rules, some of which were clearly tongue-in-cheek. They stated (The Richmond Golf Club 2018):

1. Players are asked to collect bomb and shrapnel splinters to save these causing damage to the mowing machines.
2. In competitions, during gunfire or while bombs are falling, players may take cover without penalty for ceasing play.
3. The positions of known delayed action bombs are marked by red flags at a reasonably, but not guaranteed, safe distance therefrom.
4. Shrapnel and/or bomb splinters on the fairways, or in bunkers within a club's length of a ball, may

be moved without penalty, and no penalty shall be incurred if a ball is thereby caused to move accidentally.

5. A ball moved by enemy action may be replaced, or if lost or destroyed, a ball may be dropped not nearer the hole without penalty.

6. A ball lying in a crater may be lifted and dropped not nearer the hole, preserving the line to the hole, without penalty.

7. A player whose stroke is affected by the simultaneous explosion of a bomb may play another ball from the same place. Penalty one stroke.

According to today's Richmond Golf Club members, the rules were widely publicized and even attracted the attention of Joseph Goebbels—Hitler's Minister of Propaganda, who used them as the theme of a broadcast. Goebbels uttered, "By means of these ridiculous reforms the English snobs try to impress the people with a kind of pretended heroism. They can do so without danger, because, as everyone knows, the German Air Force devotes itself only to the destruction of military targets and objectives of importance to the war effort." In fact, reports the Club, soon after, the Club's laundry was destroyed by another bombing raid.

Despite the Club's tongue-in-cheek claims, golf suffered a significant hiatus during the Second World War. In the

UK, the Open Championship was forced to take a six-year hiatus. The rest of the world suffered much the same fate, and in the US, golf, which came to be seen as a much-needed pastime and stress reliever, took a backseat to the dramatic events that followed the bombing of Pearl Harbor in December 1941.

As the bombs rained down, the commander-in-chief of the Navy's Pacific Fleet, Husband E. Kimmel, was getting dressed for his usual Sunday morning golf game at the Fort Shafter golf course. He never did make it to his golf club, yet the 2011 film, Pearl Harbor, placed him on the course at the time of the attacks. The movie seemed to suggest that Kimmel should be blamed for a lack of preparedness and strategy. In fact, Kimmel had pointed out the likelihood of a surprise attack on Pearl Harbor in February 1941. Despite this fact, he was relieved of his command a little over a week after the attack. The Roberts Commission, appointed by President Roosevelt to investigate the bombings, concluded that Kimmel had shown judgment errors and had refused to fulfill his role as commander.

The utility of the sport for boosting morale and keeping soldiers physically fit did not go unnoticed. John Kelly, the assistant director of civilian defense and a proud member of the Bala Golf Club in Philadelphia, was known for his swift playing style. Days after the Pearl Harbor bombings, he wrote to the USGA, "Eight million people will be going into the armed forces. My job is to look after the 124 million who won't or can't go. They can keep fit by playing golf. France was the most physically inactive country in the world, and look what happened to them." (Shipnuck 2020).

Kelly put his money where his mouth was, creating the position of golf deputy—a post he assigned to Fred Corcoran, manager of the PGA Tournament Bureau. They organized a series of fundraisers and, almost 20 days after the attack, Kelly wrote to the media as well as to a string of golf associations. He passionately stated that golf was key for the physical and mental well-being of Americans in times of war. He insisted, "Golf's strong attraction as a sport in which more than 2 1/4 million of our citizens exercise regularly in the open air qualifies the game for national service of a vital character. Therefore, we are urging the golf clubs and organizations of America to exert themselves to meet the requirements of individual and collective physical fitness." As was the case in the US, many British golf clubs continued to operate and permit play throughout the war.

Interestingly, those who "stayed calm and carried on play-ing" were able to do so with the confidence of knowing that their chosen sport was government-backed. Kelly hit the nail on the head when it comes to the many benefits of golf for one's physical and mental health. Today, over 25 million Americans play the sport, and the number one reason they give for sticking to it is: "mental well-being." (Gregory 2023). It is no wonder, then, that in the toughest of times, millions of men and women have turned to this sport to get their bearings, connect with nature, and focus fully on the beauty of the game.

7

CHARLIE SIFFORD: PAVING THE WAY FOR DIVERSITY

> *"I knew what I was getting into when I chose golf. Hell, I knew I'd never get rich and famous. All the discrimination, the not being able to play where I deserved and wanted to play—in the end, I didn't give a damn. I was made for a tough life because I'm a tough man. And in the end, I won: I got a lot of black people playing golf."*
>
> — CHARLIE SIFFORD

D espite the fact that golf is currently played by some 66.6 million people globally, it is still seen as an elite sport and one that still has some way to go in terms of diversity and inclusivity. As noted by writer Troy Dixon (2017), it continues to be referred to as a "gentleman's game" and it carries many upper-class connotations and stereotypes—including the idea that it is only for the rich and idle.

Golf conjures up the idea of cliquey country clubs, with gates only open to those from a specific class, race, and influence. However, today, the sport is growing in diversity, with 20% of players being people of color, and the proportion growing larger at a fast pace. More women are playing, too. According to Front Office Sports, women are fuelling the growth of the sport. Some 37% of new golfers in 2021 were women, and there are now over 6.2 million women golfers in the US. What's more, the future looks bright! Around 36% of today's junior golfers are women (Rothman 2022).

This brighter, more inclusive panorama was far from the norm in the US of the 1930s, when African-American champ, Charlie Sifford, started in the game. He learned to play while working as a caddie at a segregated club in his native North Carolina. He started smoking cigars at the age of 13, and he would play golf on Mondays—the one day that caddies were allowed on the course. He used to sneak in on other days, and credits this habit with his "poor putting" skills. Charlie said, "I was always moving fast to keep from being thrown off. I never learned to take my time on the greens and develop a good stroke."

He tried incessantly to compete on the PGA tour. He had won many "black tournaments," but had his eye on the big prize: the PGA. He was denied access year after year owing to the PGA's "Caucasian clause," which required all members to be white (Schudel 2015).

In 1960, California attorney general, Stanley Mosk, began pressuring the PGA to remove the race barrier, threatening to ban the association from competing in various areas if they didn't accede. Finally, in 1961, the PGA agreed and paved the way for Charlie to show what he was made of.

Charlie had many victories under his belt—including 4 National Black Open wins, but he was already in his late 30s when he was accepted into the PGA. For some, his chance had come too late, as he was already past his prime. However, he accepted the opportunity with characteristic vitality and took on some of golf's biggest stars at the time, including Billy Casper, Gene Littler, and Jay Hebert. He defeated Eric Monti in a sudden-death playoff, showing he had nerves of steel. In 1967, he won the Greater Hartford Open Invitational, becoming the first minority player to win a PGA Tour event. In 1969, he reigned supreme at the LA Open, joining greats like Hogan, Casper, Palmer, and Snead.

Charlie Sifford's influence on the golfing world cannot be overstated. Tiger Woods has said that he might not have ever become a professional golfer had it not been for Sifford. In 2015, the year Sifford passed away (at the ripe old age of 92!) Woods says, "He's like my grandpa that I never had. And it's been a long night and it's going to be a long few days. He fought, and what he did, the courage it took for him to stick with it and be out here and play... I probably wouldn't be here. My dad would never have picked up the game. Who knows if the clause would still exist or not? But he broke it down." (Golf Digest 2015).

Charlie Sifford was inducted into the World Golf Hall of Fame in 2004. In 2021, this organization created the Charlie Sifford Award, to honor recipients who had advanced diversity in golf. The inaugural recipient was Renee Powell, one of the most resilient athletes of our time. In 1967, she became the second African-American woman to compete on the LPGA Tour (Clearview Golf Club, n.d..). She has competed in over 250 professional tournaments and has dedicated her entire life to expanding golf to more women, minorities, seniors, youths, and military veterans.

Reflecting on his father's role in the history of golf, Charlie's son, Charles Jr., said, "Dad just wanted to play golf, but in the process, he helped open doors for others, which was important to him as well. His life story is an essential part of racial and social justice movements – then and now. It offers an opportunity to reflect on humanitarianism and the Black American experience." (Louis 2021).

Even in his late 80s, Charlie continued to be a pioneer for change. In 2009, he lent his name to a special exemption, given at the Northern Trust open in Los Angeles, where he had been triumphant 40 years previously. The recipient of the exemption was Vincent Johnson, who played in his first PGA Tour in honor of Sifford. He was delighted to be "giving someone a chance," and wished the exemption had started earlier (Harig 2009).

Charlie Sifford was a grateful man; one who learned from others to stay focused and to stop his determination from faltering. He credits good friends like Jackie Robinson for his relentless pursuit of his passion. He said, "Jackie Robinson did a beautiful job. He was my friend. When I tried to start playing, I went to Jackie Robinson and asked him about it. He asked me if I was a quitter and I said no. He said, 'If you're not a quitter, take a shot at it. But you'll run into a lot of obstacles.'"

He may have started late on the PTA tour, but his career has been no less than stellar—as has his impact on the game. As so eloquently put by Lee Elder (the first African-American to play in Masters, "Without Charlie Sifford, there would have been no one to fight the system for the blacks that followed. It took a special person to take the things that he took: the tournaments that barred him, the black cats in his bed, the hotels where he couldn't stay, the country club grills where he couldn't eat. Charlie was tough and hard. That's the reason you still see that hardness."

8

AGAINST ALL ODDS

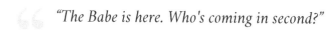

"The Babe is here. Who's coming in second?"

— BABE DIDRIKSON ZAHARIAS

W e've celebrated many great men so far, and now it's time to delve a little into women's golf. In Chapter Seven, we highlighted the fact that women are currently considered the key drivers of the game's growth. In the year 2021, the National Golf Federation (NGF) reported that the percentage of women on the greens rose to 25%, a 6% rise within just a decade. And the lockdowns of 2020 only served to amplify this trend.

According to the NGF, the progress in women's golf has been driven, in no small part, by junior development programs aimed at females. Today, girls represent 38% of all players under the age of 18. When the federation first started tracking golfing statistics, only 14% of golfers were girls (Ryan 2023).

Efforts have also been made to make golf more accessible to players of all pocket sizes. For instance, the LPGA has teamed up with big companies like Walmart to offer entry-level clubs for women. A junior player can get their hands on a full set for just $99, which is a great incentive to get on a course for the first time. Women are also bagging bigger prizes. In July 2023, 25-year-old Hawaiian whiz, Allisen Corpuz, netted $2 million—the largest prize ever for an LPGA major champion.

But let's turn back the hands of time and focus on one woman, who paved the way for current greats. She is Babe Didrikson Zaharias—one of golf's GOATs and as fine an example of courage as you could imagine. From her earliest years, she was well aware of her destiny, stating, "Before I was in my teens, I knew exactly what I wanted to be: I wanted to be the best athlete who ever lived."

Babe was born in 1911 in Port Arthur, Texas—the sixth of seven children of Norwegian immigrants. Her mother, Hannah, took in laundry, while her father, Ole, made furniture and worked at sea (Michals 2015). As you will see, golf was far from her only passion. In fact, she began an amateur sports career playing baseball in 1915, and she was such a great hitter that she earned the nickname "Babe" (after legendary baseball player, Babe Ruth).

She was a true all-rounder. She shone in every sport she played and, after reading about the 1928 Olympics, vowed she would one day go for a medal in track and field. Joined by her sister, she self-trained daily, jumping over hedges in her neighborhood. At the trials for the Olympics, she qualified for five events, but women were allowed to compete in a maximum of three.

Babe gave a stellar performance at the 1932 Olympics, winning a gold medal for the javelin throw and setting a new world record. She again took gold the next day in the 80-meter hurdle, and a silver for the high-jump.

Despite these amazing feats, she is best known for forging a path for women in golf. She started playing in 1935 and was initially discriminated against, but her wins soon led others to take note of her excellence. At the 1938 Los Angeles Open, Babe met the man who would become her husband and manager—George Zaharias, a 235-wrestler with an unwavering belief in his wife. George was as gregarious as he was intelligent, and when he met Babe, he was already making a fortune in wrestling as the "Weeping Greek from Cripple Creek."

In 1935, the US Golf Association deemed Babe to be a pro, simply because she had competed professionally in other sports. She was reinstated as an amateur in 1943, and won over 17 tournaments over the following four years. She was also the first American Woman to take home the British Amateur. She won 55 tournament victories in total, including three US Women's Opens. In 1949, she founded the Ladies Professional Golf Association.

When asked how she was able to regularly drive the ball some 250 yards when she barely weighed 145 pounds, she answered, "You've got to loosen your girdle and let it rip." Babe dominated her sport for years on end and was deemed AP's Female Athlete of the Year from 1945 to 1947 (Schwartz, n.d.). In 1948, she won her first U.S. Women's Open, as well as the World Championship and the All-American Open. She continued to dominate the LPGA Tours for the next few years.

Babe had to put down with a fair few put-downs, including that of sports writer, Joe Williams, who wrote, "It would be much better if she and her ilk stayed at home, got themselves prettied up and waited for the phone to ring." She had many more important things to think about than looking pretty. As noted by writers William Johnson and Nancy Williamson (1977), "She was an athlete and her body was her most valuable possession."

She was as highly praised as she was put down, with writers like Grantland Rice extolling her virtues thus: "She is beyond all belief until you see her perform. Then you finally understand that you are looking at the most flawless section of muscle harmony, of complete mental and physical coordination, the world of sport has ever seen."

Babe's biggest challenge came in 1953, right after winning the first edition of the Babe Zaharias Open in Beaumont: she was diagnosed with cancer. Her tumor was surgically removed, but doctors discovered the cancer had spread into her lymph nodes. A little over three months after her surgery, she made her comeback, winning her third US Women's Open by 12 strokes, subsequently raking in five titles and her sixth AP Female Athlete of the Year award. In her final years as a pro, she was reportedly bagging $100,000 a year from tournaments and endorsements (equivalent to around $1 million today).

She continued to play until spinal pain, caused by her disease, became too much to bear. In 1956, she passed away at the age of 45. Babe remains a true inspiration not only for women, but indeed for anyone who refuses to be pigeonholed. She summed up her inspiring life and career with the words, "You can't win them all—but you can try."

9

THE MIRACLE AT MEDINAH

"What impressed most in Seve was his strength, his fighting spirit, and the passion he put into every-thing he did. The best tribute we can pay to Seve is to go on playing for him, although no tribute will ever do justice to everything he did for golf and to everything he gave us."

— JOSÉ MARÍA OLAZÁBAL

Seve Ballesteros and José María Olazábal have been deemed the very best partnership in Ryder Cup history, with the Spanish duo having won 12 points in their 15 outings together. If you are already a golfing fan, then you will already know that the Ryder Cup, which is a US vs Europe competition (12 vs 12 players), has quite a special format. Specifically, the first two days of the competition include one four-match session of four-ball and one four-match session of foursomes. The final day features 12 singles matches.

In four-ball, each player in a two-man team plays his own ball. In other words, each hole involves four balls in play. Every team counties the lowest of its two scores on each hole, and the team whose player has the lowest score wins the hole. If the low scores are tied, then "half the hole" is credited to each player.

If foursomes, each two-man team plays one ball per hole, with the players taking turns until each hole is done. Players also take alternate tee shots. One is responsible for the even-numbered holes, and the other for the odd ones. Once again, in the case of a tie, the hole is halved.

In singles, every match has one player from each team. The player with the lowest score on each hole wins it. If the players tie, the hole is halved.

There are three days of play and 28 matches in total, each of which is worth one point. To win, a team must win 14 ½ of the 28 possible points. In the case of a 14-14 tie, the winning team from the previous Cup takes the trophy home (Ryder Cup, n.d.).

Seve and José María were part of "the Spanish Armada"— a talented group of Spanish players who cut an enviable swathe through the European Tour in the late 1970s and 1980s. Barely one percent of the Spanish population are regular golfers, making their victories even more impressive.

Seve, who died in 2011 from a brain tumor, was the undisputed leader of the Spanish Armada. Miguel Ángel Jiménez recalls, "He was the driving force. He was half the team and all of its soul. He went out of his way to help everyone." (Morenilla 2018). Such was his influence that in 1989, the entire team was dressed in their uniforms for the official team photo—except Seve, who arrived in unofficial attire. Player Sam Torrance turned to the captain, Tony Jacklin, and asked, "Does this mean all of us have to change?"

1985, says Manuel Piñero (another member of the Spanish Armada) was the year that the Spanish lost their "inferiority complex." Manuel recalls playing alongside Seve and fighting back the emotions welling up inside him as he heard the English screaming, "Viva España ("Long live Spain")." He turned to Seve and said, "If this keeps up, I won't be able to continue playing." And he was determined to do his best for a man he admired so much.

As close as he was to other players, Seve's golfing soul-mate was undoubtedly José María Olazábal, who joined the team in 1987, literally "quaking in his shoes." He still recalls how Seve calmed his frazzled nerves the first time they played together, saying, "You play your game, and I'll deal with the rest." These words, he said, were exactly what he needed to play a game that would see Europe finally win on American soil.

But we've veered far from our story, which centers on Europe's miracle at the Medinah Country Club (in Illinois) in 2012, inspired by Seve Ballesteros. This match was deemed one of the most amazing comebacks in the history of golf, and it featured Ian Poulter and José María Olazábal. This was the first Ryder Cup since Seve's death the year previous, and José María took on the role of Captain for the European team. What happened that day had never happened before in Ryder Cup history: José María's side was down 10-4 on Saturday, yet they won eight of the last day's singles, earning a shocking outright victory when Francesco Molinari halved with Tiger Woods in the 28th, turning the match into a thrilling battle.

It has been an exciting and unpredictable match through-out. Europe struggled badly on the first two days, but shone in the singles, with Luke Donald scoring a win over Masters champion Bubba Watson, Paul Lawrie beating Brandt Snedeker, and Rory McIlroy reigning supreme over the previously undefeated Keegan Bradley.

Europe's fifth victory in six matches against the US was achieved in Seve's colors, and they wore images of him on their sleeves and bags. Their inspiration was Seve's fighting spirit, though the man himself had never been called upon to make such a shocking comeback.

At the press conference, José María, who was visibly filled with emotion, told the press, "Seve will always be present…it's the first time that he's not here with us at the Ryder Cup. I do have wonderful memories from my matches with him." José María openly spoke of how close Seve was to his heart, and that when the team met to discuss the day's play, their former captain was very much on every player's mind. (Sky Sports 2020).

Manuel Piñero hit the nail on the head when he said, "Golf cannot be understood without Severiano Ballesteros nor probably Seve without golf, his life, his passion. In my opinion, there have been three legends in the history of golf: Bobby Jones, Ben Hogan, and Severiano Ballesteros. Each one in his time and style, but the three of them are essential to understand the development of this sport." (Seve Ballesteros, n.d.).

10

INVENTING DRAMA

"Golfers should not fail to realize that it is a game of great traditions, of high ideals of sportsmanship, one in which a strict adherence to the rules is essential."

— FRANCIS OUIMET

There is nothing sports fans enjoy more than the triumph of the underdog, and the subplots of this seemingly simple story are what make it so fascinating. The plot revolves around Francis Ouimet, a 20-year-old caddie who lived across the street from The Country Club in Brookline, Massachusetts, where the Open was being contested in 1913. Ouimet had grown up in challenging economic circumstances and was working at a local sporting goods store.

In the year of this fateful Open, Harry Vardon was the biggest name in golf at the time. Hailing from the British Crown Dependency of the Isle of Jersey, he was the winner of five British Opens and one US Open (Tays 2013). Vardon was touring the US with fellow player, Ted Ray, and the USGA had agreed to postpone the Open until September so the two stars could make it—something previously unheard-of in US golf.

Ouimet, meanwhile, was a young man who had made a bit of a name for himself over the previous three years, having missed out on qualifying for the US Amateur by only one shot. In 1913, he was victorious at the Massachusetts Amateur and managed to qualify for the US Amateur (although he lost out to Jerome Travers).

The then-President of the USGA, Robert Watson, decided to enter Ouimet in the US Open without asking the young player, as he was looking for a talented amateur to add to the list of seasoned players. Of course, nobody expected Ouimet to do well, as it was assumed that the victory would go to either Vardon or Ray. These champs were unaware that Ouimet lived a stone's throw away from Brookline, but it can confidently be said that had they known, it wouldn't have made a difference. They boasted all the experience that the young man lacked, and had their sights set on other competitors.

Before the Open commenced, players competed in two qualifying rounds. Half the golfers played on Tuesday, the second half on Wednesday, and the top 32 golfers from each day would qualify for the tournament, which would comprise 36 holes on Thursday and Friday.

Close to the Open, the Boston Journal elaborated, "Not since a championship was first played in this country has it been necessary for the association to hold qualifying rounds, but this year, with Vardon, Ray, and Reid from England, and Louis Tellier from France, added interest has been taken, with the result that a record-breaking field entered." (Coggeshall 2013). An article published in Salt Lake City's Evening Telegram, meanwhile, highlighted the participation of many talented amateurs—but omitted Ouimet.

On Day 1 of the qualifying round, Ouimet came in second at 74-78–152, behind Vardon (who scored 75-76–151). By the end of the second qualifying round, Ted Ray led all qualifiers with a 36-hole course record 74-74–148, and Ouimet achieved the fifth-best qualifying score.

And on to the tournament they went! On September 19, the Morning Oregonian praised English players, Vardon and Reid, who turned in cards of 147 for the first 36 holes, taking the lead by two strokes. They were followed by Edward Ray and Herbert Strong, who scored 149. Francis Ouimet turned in a card of 151, which placed him in a tie for fourth place.

Two rounds and one day of play were left, and Ouimet did the unthinkable, tying with Ray and Vardon! The

Colorado Springs Gazette marveled at how a young American, "a stripling scarcely out of his teens," had made sporting history. The Gazette noted that when the spectators realized that an amateur from the local area had a chance of winning the championship, "they lost that placid attitude that ordinarily marks the golf galleries and rooted and cheered Ouimet in a manner typical of baseball and football games. The scenes that attended Ouimet's march over the last four holes have never been equaled on an American or European golf course."

The 18th hole was particularly exciting, as Ouimet needed to hole out in one (to win) or two (for a tie). He made a 35-foot putt that barely missed the hole, rolling around three feet past it. With a second, gentle tap, the ball was in. It dropped in for the 4, tying him with Ray and Vardon. The crowd went wild and swept past ropes and cards, lifting Ouimet off his shoulders and carrying him towards the clubhouse, a loud cheer accompanying the entire journey. The Gazette reported that Ouimet was "surrounded by several thousand cheering, yelling golfers who forgot their golf in the enthusiasm of being just Americans cheering an American victory." (Blumenthal 2020).

The tie led to a final day, during which an exciting 18-hole playoff took place. Ouimet was victorious, scoring 72—a whopping 5 strokes less than Vardon and 6 less than Ray. On September 21, the Sunday Herald published a photo of Ouimet being carried off the course by the spectators, hailing his victory over Vardon and Ray as an unparalleled and well-deserved triumph: "It was a victory for an amateur that is unprecedented in the history of competitive golf."

Another big hero of the match was Eddie Lowery, who was only 10 when he caddied for Ouimet at the 1913 event. Ouimet wrote for The American Golfer: "My little caddie, Eddie Lowery … not much bigger than a peanut, was a veritable inspiration all around…(his) influence on my game I cannot overestimate."

It was pure coincidence that led Eddie to caddie for Ouimet. Eddie and his brother Jack played hooky on Thursday—the day on which the first two rounds of the US Open were taking place. However, Jack got caught and sent back to school. Eddie, however, made a lucky escape and made his way to The Country Club. When he offered to caddy for Ouimet, the latter said, "Eddie, you're shorter than my bag, you can't do this." But Eddie showed dogged determination and managed to convince Ouimet that he was the right guy for the job (Mosier 2013)!

Ouimet's victory was described as being entirely merited. Despite thousands of spectators surrounding him, wrote the Herald, he remained unfazed, going hole after hole with the eye of a supreme strategist and throwing him off his game with his "heart of oak and nerves of steel."

It is difficult to quantify the extent to which Ouimet's victory inspired Americans, many of whom took up golf for the first time after having a home-grown hero to look up to. Ouimet continued to play golf as an amateur, successfully defending his Massachusetts Amateur title and then winning a US Amateur tournament. He won the Amateur title again in 1931 and in 1951, he became the first non-British Captain of the Royal and Ancient Golf Club of St. Andrews. He went on to become a banker and stockbroker and his caddy, Eddie, a millionaire business-man. Many years after the Open, Ouimet and Eddie spoke to sports writer, Grantland Rice. Eddie recalls that on the day of the match, Vardon was visibly cracking under the strain, while Ouimet remained cool and calm, "as if he were playing a dime Nassau with two old pals."

11

THE 1999 US OPEN: A CLASH OF GENERATIONS

"But in the end, it's still a game of golf, and if at the end of the day you can't shake hands with your opponents and still be friends, then you've missed the point."

— PAYNE STEWART

The 1999 US Open is considered a pivot point between golf icons of the 1990s and the future stars of the 2000s, all of whom fought to the bitter end. It highlights the factors that make the US Open so special—including the fact that it takes place over some of the nation's most difficult courses.

The 1999 Open was the first to be played at Pinehurst #2 —one of the most famous and historically rich courses in the world. Golf.com contributor, Zephyr Melton, once wrote that he had never played on a course "with such tormenting green complexes" (2020) and this challenging layout only added to the excitement of the game.

Built in 1907 and designed by Donald Ross, Pinehurst #2 boasts unique undulations and shaping of the greens. Ross was known for designing exceptionally difficult green complexes, but this course is often said to be his best creation. Many of its greens are crowned, causing shots that are short to roll off the green and making chip shots more difficult. Johnny Miller hit the nail on the head when he said that trying to sink a ball on a Pinehurst green was "like trying to hit a ball on top of a VW Beetle." (Smith, n.d.).

At the 1999 Open, Payne Stewart and Lee Janzen were the consolidated stars, while Phil Mickelson, David Duvall, and Tiger Woods were getting ready to take over. At the time, Woods had a 1997 Masters under his belt, but he had his share of doubters. Duvall, meanwhile, was the world number one after completing a top-notch season. Mickelson was also shining bright and was known in the circle as the "best golfer to never win a major." Janzen had won the Open the year before, while Stewart had been victorious the year before that.

Stewart hoped to cap off 1990, his "comeback year," with a victory at the Open. He had been a rising star at the age of 34, having won the 1991 Open. However, a couple of years after his victory, he was offered a big monetary deal by Spalding that required him to play with a set of clubs that were ill-suited to his style. They forced him to develop a series of compensating moves that served him poorly under pressure. Over the next four seasons, he made the top 10 a whopping 28 times, but managed only one win.

Stewart's struggles ushered in an era of deep introspection—one in which he decided to dedicate more time to his children and deal with the loss of his best friend to cancer. During this time, he contemplated his own mortality. His faith—both in his religion and himself—deepened and by 1998, he was playing with his old clubs and ready to show the world what he could do. Prior to his dry spell, he had been known for a swing so beautiful it was often described in culinary terms—including "buttery" and "syrupy." (Shipnuck 2014). Stewart's good looks were matched by his charismatic personality. He could be dry with fellow players, but he was also known as a great host and the life of the party—a master margarita mixologist who was as loyal as he was sincere.

When the Open rolled up, he felt readier than ever to do one thing: make history at Pinehurst.

The first day of the competition was rainy—a fact that worked in the favor of players, who found that the wet grass made the course a little less inhospitable. By the end of the day, Mickelson and Duvall were in the lead with a score of 67, while Woods and Stewart had shot

68. Janzen, meanwhile, didn't have a great day, scoring 74.

In round two, conditions remained favorable, and the scores were still close. Duvall and Mickelson had both shot even par rounds to score 70, while Duvall took the lead at 69. Woods had dropped a stroke, but was still only 2 behind Stewart.

On Day Three, Stewart was still ahead. He opened up a one-stroke lead despite difficult conditions, ending the day with a score of 72. The sun was up in the sky and this led even the best players (including Stewart) to shoot over par. Mickelson managed to even par, but was still in second place. Wood was two shots behind the leader, but Duvall began to lag behind, with a round of 75. By the end of the third day, the top scores were: Payne Stewart at 68-69-72-70, Phil Mickelson at 67-70-73-70, and Tiger Woods at 68-71-72-70.

The final day was looking good for Stewart, but memories of the previous US Open (in which he lost out to Janzen) lingered. At that match, Stewart had been leading by 4 strokes entering the final round. However, Janzen managed to play a better game, and Stewart was crushed by the defeat.

This time, Stewart was going at it with Mickelson, and the day was filled with challenges. Stewart drove a nasty lie in the right rough on the long par -4 hole and was forced to pitch out. The bogey gave Mickelson a 1-stroke lead. At number 14, Woods drained a 30-footer for a birdie, pumping his fist and sending the crowd into a frenzy. According to Mickelson, you could feel the tension building, and both he and Stewart knew that Tiger wasn't going to give up without a good fight.

By the 16th hole, Woods was within one stroke of the lead. The pressure got to Stewart, who bogeyed the 15th, tying now with Woods. Tiger had to land a five-foot putt to save par on the 17th hole, but missed, and the victory now looked like it belonged to Mickelson.

Meanwhile, Stewart needed to sink a 30-footer just to save par on hole 16. He drained it and managed to stay one stroke back, while Mickelson missed his own par putt and this meant that the two were now tied!

On the 17th, Mickelson missed a short putt and Stewart drained his birdie. Suddenly, the narrative had flipped and there was only one hole left. On the par 4 18th hole, Stewart started with a poor drive but gave it his all and got on the green in three shots. Mickelson needed a 30-foot putt for birdie but missed it by a bit. Stewart drained an 18-foot putt and victory was his!

The 1999 US Open is often referred to in golf literature as, quite, simply, "The Greatest US Open ever." (Shipnuck 2014).

It is difficult to leave that this was Stewart's last victory ever. He died in a plane crash a few months later, leaving the golfing world with a hole that could never be filled. According to the National Transportation Safety Board, the aircraft had failed to pressurize, incapacitating the crew with hypoxia. The plane soared through the sky on autopilot until it ran out of fuel and crashed (Kiner 2019).

Like Seve Ballesteros, Stewart was a well-loved figure in golf who was considered the heart and soul of the Ryder Cup during the fierce feuds of the late 1980s and 1990s. Stewart had 11 wins on the PGA Tour, 1 on the European Tour, 1 on the Japan tour, and 11 others. In addition to his Open wins, he was also victorious at the PGA Championship in 1989. He additionally represented his country on five Ryder Cup teams and played for the US on three World Cup teams.

His biography on the World Golf Hall of Fame website reads, "Payne Stewart will be remembered for many achievements. But Stewart had one of the most stylish swings of the modern era. It was not the structured action of many of today's players, but rather a long and wonderfully graceful and fluid movement. Stewart's clothes were as stylish as his swing. His outlandish plus-fours, tams, and elegant outfits make him unmistakable on the course." (Kiner 2019).

12

A TALE OF RESILIENCE AND REDEMPTION

 "I'm a fighter. I'm a survivor, and I'll get through anything people can throw at me."

— JOHN DALY

John Daly was a 5x PGA Tour winner who earned the nickname "Long John" when he burst onto the Tour because he could hit the ball further than any of his competitors. In 1997, he became the first-ever PGA Tour player to average over 300 yards per drive over a full season!

His life was filled with as many lucky breaks as tragedies. It is often said that he was given one very lucky break on the day he won the 1991 PGA Championship. Back then, Daly was 25 and was listed as the ninth alternate for the major. He essentially had next to no chance of being called to play.

With little more than 12 hours until his tee off in Indiana, he was some 500 miles away at his Germantown home in Tennessee. The phone rang, and it was Nick Price—a well-known PGA Tour star with three wins to his name. The Zimbabwean rang Daly in desperation, as his wife was about to give birth, and he had to pull out last minute.

Daly drove through the night, landing in Carmel early Thursday morning. He had a place on the field, but few thought he could pose a threat, let alone take home the coveted prize! At the time, it had been four years since Daly turned pro, but he failed to shine on the PGA Tour. What's more, in the 1991 championship, he was up against three of the biggest games in the history of golf— Seve Ballesteros, Nick Faldo, and Payne Stewart.

Daly, who sported his characteristic mullet on the big day, had never even played a single hole at Crooked Hill. Thankfully, Price lent him a hand in the form of his caddie, Jeff Medlin, who offered his guidance to the newbie.

Daly may not have drawn the same crowds that year as Ballesteros or Faldo, but, as reported by fellow PGA Tour pro Bobby Clampett, Daly was already a bit of a legend because of the raw power of his hit. Clampett, captured the essence of what made Daly so special: "John's the ulti- mate feel player. He sometimes doesn't make the wisest decisions of strategy on the golf course – he just goes with how he feels."

That day, it was pretty evident that Daly was in "the Zone." Golfer, Trevor Immelman, recalls how Wild John's vigorous style made him a huge favorite among spectators. "You see this guy that was playing golf like we had never seen before from a standpoint of playing so free and hitting it so far and really changing the dynamics of how this golf course was supposed to be played." (Bantock 2023).

By the end of the third round (on Saturday), Daly was leading by three strokes over fellow Americans, Kenny Knox and Craig Stadler. With one day left to the final day, most players made it a point to rest, refuel, and gather energy. Daly, by contrast, headed to kick a field goal for the Indianapolis Colts during a pre-season game at Hoosier Dome. His kick was so straight and impressive, that he was invited to kick again the following week (Bantock 2023)!

Clampett recalls Daly asking him what to do on the last day as they walked down the fairway. His advice was to play for the crowd and enjoy every shot—and the player did just that, egging the spectators on and building a beautiful, positive synergy that lasted until the final hole. He carded 12-under, beating Bruce Lietzke by three shots. His final score was an incredible 69-67-69-71—276. That day, Daly became a superstar, and he commenced a brilliant though sometimes erratic career that would go down in history as one of the most brilliant and unique.

On one fateful day in 1997, Daly was ready to call it quits. He drove his Mercedes to the edge of a cliff in Palm Springs. He was contemplating ending his own life. Years of addiction, coupled with the pressures of success, had taken their toll.

In the humorous yet emotion-packed documentary *Hit it Hard*, which contains a plethora of incredible anecdotes, quotes, and stories about Daly, it was revealed that the man who saved him from taking the fateful plunge was former Dallas Cowboys player, Thomas "Hollywood" Henderson. The footballer recalled that he was in his bed resting when his phone rang. He could hear an engine roaring and the sound of Daly's voice. The golfer was upset and told him that he was about to end his life. Henderson burst into tears. He begged Daly not to go ahead with his plans, saying, "The world ain't done with John Daly." He told his friend that he had never asked him for a single favor but tonight, he had a big one to ask: for Daly to go home. Luckily, the golfer decided to take Henderson's advice, and keep fighting (Porter 2016).

Daly admitted to the New York Post that the reason behind his depression was his fight to see his child, Shynah. The PGA Tour was insisting he go to rehab, and he was having a hard time doing something he didn't want to. He admits that he wasn't used to such a high level of success, and it took him time to adapt to it. He stated, "I've screwed up a lot, but I've always admitted it," Daly told *The Post*. "Looking at my downs in life, it's incredible that I'm still here, to be honest with you. I never thought I'd see 50." (Cannizzaro 2016).

There were many moments of light in John Daly's life, and many were filled with friendship and laughter. Like the time in 2008 when he showed off a golf course in Missouri that bears his name. He greeted the reporter shirtless and shoeless—an attitude that led "the Wild Child" to be reprimanded by the head of the PGA (not that he cared)! Or the time he decided it was time to shed a few pounds—and he went on a diet of popcorn and Jack Daniels!

One of the most characteristic Daly traits is his passion for odd fashion on the field—to be specific, his penchant for wearing pants featuring silhouetted figures of naked women. And of course, a classic Daly tale is the time he won $55,000 at a casino and threw it away. As a guest on the Dan Le Batard Show, he told the interviewer that he had been arguing with his wife in the car when he decided to throw all the money out of the window!

If anyone else told you this story, you probably wouldn't believe them, but when it comes to John Daly, truth is certainly more enticing than fiction. And there is no better story than a life as fully lived as his.

13

GOLF ON THE MOON

"I can hit it farther on the moon. But actually, my swing is better here on Earth."

— ALAN SHEPARD

The love of golf knows no bounds, and truly keen players will play just about anywhere where they can swing a club—including the moon! As mind-boggling as this may seem, it actually happened on February 6, 1971, when Alan Shepard, the commander of the Apollo 14 mission to the moon, took "a little white pellet that's familiar to millions of Americans" and decided to have some fun. He hit a total of two golf balls from the lunar surface, using a makeshift 6-iron he had hidden away in the space capsule.

Shepherd was an avid golfer who had asked Jack Harden, a club pro at River Oaks Country Club in Texas, to build him the special club. The astronaut tucked the club in his spacesuit during the launch, alongside a few golf balls hidden in his sock.

It was an act of true rebellion, since none of the items were on NASA's inventory. The Apollo program had cost close to $25 billion, and scheduled activities were meticulously planned to make the most of the astronauts' time on the moon. Shepherd did run it by the mission director, Bob Gilruth, who agreed to the astronaut's whim, so long as play was limited to the end of extravehicular activities —and only if there was enough time left!

Shepard worked patiently for nine hours and, on his way back to the lunar module, he knew it was his moment. He attached the modified club head to a tool used to scoop lunar rock samples and navigated one of the universe's most unique bunkers one-handed (Bantock 2023).

The sheer weight of his spacesuit made it impossible to grip the club with both hands, so he used his right hand. He made four swings, hitting mostly moon dust on the first two. He hit a shank shot on his third attempt, and finally caught the ball flush on his fourth go. He believed the ball had gone "miles and miles and miles," but technology eventually proved him wrong.

One of the balls was found by fellow astronaut, Edgar Mitchell, in a nearby crater, just 24 yards away. The second wasn't found until half a century later, when imaging specialist, Andy Saunders, was able to digitally enhance scans of the original film taken during the expedition. He discovered that the second ball was only 40 yards away from where Shephard had made his famous shot!

Saunders wrote for the US Golfer's Association, "The fact that Shepard even made contact and got the ball airborne is extremely impressive." He told BBC Sport that practically no golfer could successfully hit a six-iron with one hand, using a quarter swing out of an unraked bunker. Much less if they were wearing a heavy suit, helmet, and gloves. And gravity, he reminded readers, should definitely be taken into account, since it exerted a downward pressure on the club head.

He did state, however, that if a professional golfer had hit the ball on the moon at around 298 kilometers per hour (a speed achieved by PGA champ Jimmy Walker) at an ideal 45° angle, the ball would have landed some 2.62 miles away. It would have remained in the air for a full minute!

Pro golfer Gary Felton, meanwhile, felt that Shepard was simply a poor golfer. He told IFL Science, "Mr. Shepard was, unfortunately, a golfer who, despite arguably ill-advised golfing attire, was a bit of a fibber. You disastrously embellished your performance on the Moon."

USGA historian, Victoria Nenno, blames Shepard's poor performance on his suit, noting that Earth-bound golfers have tech advances (like moisture-wicking clothes), which were inaccessible to Shephard in the 1970s. She is excited to hear of the new, more flexible spacesuits that NASA is creating for the Artemis program, "It would be very interesting to see how that would affect the shot," she stated (Howell 2021).

HELP TO INSPIRE OTHERS!

"Golf is about how well you accept, respond to, and score with your misses much more so than it is a game of your perfect shots."

— DR BOB ROTELLA

By this stage in your reading, you have probably come across a host of "hits and misses" and discovered how golfing greats have come back from huge handicaps, both on the golf course and in life. No matter how well you aim your swing, there are a myriad of factors that will undoubtedly make a day's play anything but predictable— the climatic conditions, the attitude of your rivals, and how you feel physically and mentally.

Despite being described as a solitary sport, golf is never just about you and your clubs. One attribute I hoped to bring out in this book is the powerful bonds, friendships, and camaraderie that take place on the golf course. The Miracle at Medinah is a perfect example of how golf's greatest players have mentored and inspired each other. The dynamic duo, Seve Ballesteros and José María Olazábal, revealed how more seasoned experts have generously passed the baton on to those who doubted their ability or became overwhelmed with doubt on the day of a big competition.

My hope throughout this book is to take you—a lover of great stories—onto the golf course for the first time—or back to your favorite club very soon if you're a seasoned player. Not only because the game itself is so enthralling, but also because of the many life lessons it has to teach—everything from maintaining your focus when the moment is tense, to bouncing back from challenges and respecting your competitors. Remember Jack Nicklaus and his famous concession, which was one of the sport's most memorable actions!

If this book is inspiring you to create a few great golf stories of your own, then I hope you can share your enthusiasm with other readers.

By leaving a review of this book on Amazon, you'll inspire others to take their first golf lesson—or find innovative new ways to improve their handicap.

Simply by leaving a short review, you'll help them find examples of sportsmanship, creativity, and innovation—all of which can inspire them to be their best selves!

Thank you so much for your support. Let's get back to the club!

Scan the QR code for a quick review!

14

THE FIRST AND ONLY CALENDAR YEAR GRAND SLAM

"Golf is the closest game to the game we call life. You get bad breaks from good shots, you get good breaks from bad shots, but you have to play where the ball lies."

— BOBBY JONES

Bobby Jones was arguably one of the best-rounded golfers of all time; a true 'Renaissance Man' who was just as comfortable with a book in his hand as he was with a club. He was born in 1902 in Atlanta. Georgia. His youth was marred by poor health, and golf was recommended to strengthen him. Bobby won his first kids' tournament at the age of six at his home course, East Lake Golf Club. His first important victory was in 1916, when he nabbed the Georgia Amateur Championship at the age of 14! His talent caught the eye of the USGA, which invited him to take part in the US Amateur in Philadelphia. He was the youngest competitor in the tournament, and he lost in the third round. The next year, however, he became the youngest player ever to win the Southern Amateur.

Bobby was as generous as he was gifted, and in 1917, he played in numerous exhibition events with fellow golfers Perry Adair, Alexa Sterling, and Elaine Rosenthal, raising more than $150,000 for the American Red Cross World War I relief effort (Bobby Jones, n.d.).

He was also an intellectual young man, who achieved degrees from Georgia Tech, Harvard, and Emory. He studied German, French, and Latin. He completed his B.S. in mechanical engineering at the Georgia Institute of Technology and in 1924, he received a degree in English literature from Harvard. Next up was Law School (Bobby's father was a prominent lawyer). After only one year at Emory University Law School, he passed the state bar exam and in 1928, was admitted to the Georgia Bar and started working at his father's law firm.

Bobby was clearly cut from a different cloth than most "mere mortals" but in 1930, he did the unthinkable— he won all of golf's major championships in the same calendar year (the British Amateur, the British Open, the US Open, and the US Amateur. Although others may have come close—for instance, Tiger Woods won four consecutive majors between 2000 and 2001, nobody thus far has achieved what Jones did (Fitzpatrick 2015).

On September 27, 1930, Jones won the US Amateur at Merion Golf Club, a feat that would later be referred to as the "Grand Slam" (its equivalent today comprises the U.S. Open, British Open, Masters, and PGA Championship.) It was fitting that the championship was being held at Merion, since it was here that he first burst on the scene as an impressive teen player.

The format consisted of a 36-hole match. After cruising through the first two 18-hole matches, he was ready to make the trophy his. In the final against Eugene Homans, he carded the equivalent of 33 on the second nine and led by 7 at the break. From then on, the crowds swelled to watch history being made. The match was effectively won at the par -4 11th hole.

Rather shockingly, Jones, then aged 28, announced his retirement from pro golf. "The strain of golf is wrecking my health, stunting me in my business ambitions, and I'm dead tired of it," he another competitor in the locker room on the day of the Grand Slam.

At the trophy presentation, he hinted at the same, telling the press that he wasn't sure if he would be playing many tournaments. At the very least, he would most likely stay out of battle in the following season. Two months later, it became official. Jones announced his retirement.

Soon after his major coup, he began a new project: building his dream golf course in Augusta. He sought advice from Clifford Roberts, who later became chairman of the club. They found the perfect spot in a 400-acre former indigo plantation, overlooked by a 14-room manor house—the first building in the South made of concrete.

Upon visiting the site, Jones felt it was right. He was fascinated by the beauty of the old manor house and the unique trees and shrubs that surrounded it. He recalls one defining moment: when he walked on the grassy area graced with tall trees behind the house, looking down at the property. He felt that this land had been waiting for years for someone to transform it into a golf course. In fact, it required minimal interference. It looked as though it was ready to be the backdrop for an exciting day's play.

His aim (and that of architect, Alister MacKenzie) was to create a private course of natural beauty that average and seasoned golfers alike would enjoy playing. He stated, "We want to make the bogeys easy, if frankly sought, pars readily obtainable by standard good play, and birdies, except on par-fives, dearly bought." The fairways were ample and the rough light, but during a tournament, the greens would speed things up and the hole locations would provide an exciting challenge (Kingdom, n.d.).

Augusta opened in 1933 and an annual event was soon established whereby the best players in the world would be invited to play. Roberts wished to call it the Masters and unofficially used this term, despite Bobby's objections (he thought it was too presumptuous). However, by 1939, the term was so widely used that Bobby had no choice but to relent! The Augusta National Invitation Tournament became known as the Masters Tournament—and it has retained this catchy name ever since! The purse for the Masters has risen considerably over the past few years and currently stands at $15 million (the winner takes home $2.7 million). (May 2023).

Today, the Masters is always celebrated on the second week of April. The Club has a strict membership of only 300 and can be played by invite only. It is sometimes referred to as the most exclusive club in the world of sports.

15

THE 1997 MASTERS—PUTTING GOLF ON THE MAP

"I think about it when I return to Augusta and remember what a cool experience it was. The tournament, the fans, hugging Pop, and seeing my mom when it was over and what it meant for the minority players that came before me. I'll never forget that week."

— TIGER WOODS

Sometimes, the significance of a victory extends beyond the size of the prize or the records being broken. This was very much the case on April 13, 1997, when Tiger Woods became the youngest player to win the coveted Masters.

His youth was only one element of what made this victory so special. He was the first African-American to play the event, and it was especially emotion-packed because his father, Earl Woods, was still in recovery from heart surgery but had made his way to Augusta to watch his son make history. Earl, a former US Army infantry officer who served two tours of duty in Vietnam and achieved the rank of lieutenant colonel, had learned to play golf in the 1970s, at the age of 42. He coached his son Tiger, who quickly became a child prodigy and honed his craft on southern California's military courses.

The world's eye was on Tiger by 1997. He had already claimed a string of amateur victories and had reigned supreme three times as a pro. However, the 1997 Masters was the event that gave rise to the legend. He shot a tournament record 18-under 270, winning by an incredible 12 strokes. This was the biggest margin of victory in any major championship, though Woods again set a new standard when he won the 2000 US Open at Pebble Beach by 15 strokes.

How can anyone leave his competitors so far behind? The answer lay in his wedges. He hit them into 11 of the 18 holes on the golf course (including the par -5 15th) and didn't three-putt a single time. He scored two eagles, 21 birdies, 42 pars, and seven bogeys. Following his four-over-par 40 on the opening nine, he fought back to pay the last 63 holes in 22 under. This led to the alleged "Tiger-proofing" of the course (it was stretched from 6,925 yards to 7,445), yet Woods has donned three more green jackets since!

In many ways, the victory was foreseeable, given the big boost he received a week before he left for Augusta, while he was playing at Isleworth with Mark O'Meara. The latter recalls that he and Tiger used to bet when they played. O'Meara could sense Tiger was stronger than ever when he was down 10 after 12 holes. Tiger shot an easy 59, fetching $65 from his good friend. He was more than ready to brave his competitors at Augusta (McDaniel, 2022).

To win such a prestigious competition by 12 shots at such a young age was unheard of, but what made it even more special was the fact that it occurred at Augusta, where black players had been denied the opportunity to play for so long.

Writing during Black History Month in 2020, writer Sean O'Brien pointed out that he was hard-pressed to think of a sporting victory that meant as much as Woods'. Black players were not allowed to compete at the Masters until the mid-1970s. Woods' achievement symbolized some-thing great for black Americans everywhere, and the player was aware of the significance of the moment.

Woods thanks three prominent black players who had paved the way for him—Charlie Sifford, Lee Elder, and Ted Rhodes. A long time before these golfers made their mark on golf history, John Shippen became the first African-American to compete at the US Open (coming in fifth in 1896). Meanwhile, George Franklin Grant, the first African-American professor at Harvard and a Boston dentist, invented the golf tee in 1899. It was made from wood and natural rubber tubing!

In a rare 1990 interview with Trans World Sport, 14-year-old Tiger told the interviewer that racism was very much still alive in the golfing world. He recalls others making him feel out of place, especially in zones in which slavery had been rife. After his 1997 victory, he appeared in a Nike ad, saying, "There are still courses in the United States that I am not allowed to play on because of the color of my skin."

Tiger was aware of what his win meant to the world, but in his memory, what really stands out is the big effort his dad had made to be there and support him. Earl's open-heart surgery had been fraught with challenges. He flat-lined and was revived. He was in an extremely delicate state, but couldn't stop himself from standing by his son on such a historic day (McDaniel 2022).

Tiger recalls going into the competition without expecta-tions of winning. The day before the final round, he had a long discussion with his dad, who warned him that Sunday would be one of the most challenging rounds he would ever play in his life. For Tiger, the victory was the fulfillment of his dreams, hard work, and consistency. To this day, he says, every time he returns to Augusta, he thinks of the Masters and what it meant to him and his family. He also remembers all the groundwork laid by minority players before him. "I'll never forget that week," he said (Rooth, n.d.).

Woods is often referred to as the Greatest of All Time by today's golfing stars. By attracting millions of spectators and new players to the sport, he can be partially credited for making it as lucrative as it is. During his career, prize money, media contracts, and brand deals grew exponentially. But Tiger's influence goes way beyond money. He is an inspiration to anyone with self-belief and the commitment to back it.

For many, the moment when Tiger walked over to his dad, embraced him tightly, and wept, was one of the most emotive in all of sporting history. And they would undoubtedly say that as great as golf has been since that symbolic day, nothing will ever match the 1997 Masters.

16

THE HARD CLIMB TO THE SUMMIT

"When you can play an entire hole swinging with 50 percent tempo, you'll begin to appreciate how many more options you have for your game."

— PIA NILSSON

Despite the incredible rise in popularity of the game of golf, it's still hard to find female coaches working with top pros, but two of them—Pia Nilsson and Lynn Marriott—learned through experience that fighting for greater equality in the sport was worth the blood, sweat, and tears. According to NBC, they are more or less the only female coaches consistently working with the PGA Tour and LPGA pros on the world's most competitive stages.

Other women indeed paved the way for women in golf. Take Susie Meyers, who has been honored by Golf Magazine as one of the Top 100 Teachers in the country. A member of The PGA of America since 1994, she has competed on the LPGA tour and played in four US Opens and one LPGA Championship. She not only teaches her students the technical aspects of the game, but also uses the Socratic Method during coaching, to bring out the student's belief in themselves and their talent. She is known for emphasizing the power of the mind and for her personalized approach to the game. "There is no perfect swing, but there is a swing for each golfer. Golf is a game to be played creatively," she has said. Meyer has coached players at the highest level, including Michael Thompson and Derek Ernst, helping them achieve important victories.

Then there is Pam Barnett, who helped her student Ted Purdy (whom she had coached since he was seven years old) play in his first Masters thanks to a top 40 finish on the 2004 PGA Tour money list. Purdy says that whenever he told people his coach was coming, they would ask, "Where is he?" Yet Barnett has coached an impressive list of touring pros and top amateurs—including Tour players Jerry Smith and Jonathan Kaye, Hall of Famer Beth Daniel, and Pia Nilsson herself.

Gale Peterson and Nancy Quarcelino are two more coaches who share their knowledge from their respective home bases. However, it can confidently be said that

Nilsson and Marriott are the most consistently present female coaches at major tour events (Mell 2020).

The dynamic duo have written various books and founded Vision54—which offers coaching programs for players and coaches. One aspect that makes their program stand out is their "focused micro-coaching" approach, designed to solve the specific challenges golfers face.

So what was the climb to the top like? Wrought with challenges!

The first time the coaches approached a New York publisher for their book, *Every Shot Must Have a Purpose*, they were told to "rewrite it as a book for women golfers." Yet they refused, answering that their message was meant for all golfers. Thankfully, a few weeks later, the publisher changed his mind.

Marriott also had to take a player aptitude test to become a member of the PGA of America. She had to play PGA National in Florida from the same tees as the men, and although it was hard to reach the fairway on some holes, she made it through. She told NBC Sports, "It was a man's world, and I knew if I was going to have any chance of pursuing what I really wanted to do, I had to have the PGA certification." (Mell 2020). It was a tough requirement and took her three attempts. She was among the first women to pass this test.

Without a doubt, one of their greatest achievement was opening their revolutionary golf school while working with three of the world's number-one players. Susan Reed, who helped the duo pen their book Be a Player, referred to them as "singular in sports in terms of women being at the top of their profession…(not just) in coaching top athletes (but) at the top of the coaching profession in understanding how athletes perform." ((Mell 2020).

When Nilsson partnered up with Marriott, she was at a crossroads in her career. She had been head coach of Sweden's national teams for a decade, and when that experience ended, she was looking for a new project. In her home country, she had achieved such good results that she was named head coach not only of the Swedish women's team but also of the entire national program. This covered men's, women's, junior, amateur, and pro teams. She recalls that despite her impressive track record (she had excelled on the LPGA for five years), there was some resentment when she was given the job. "There were questions about whether a woman could lead the men," she said.

She traces her resilience and belief in her ability to her childhood. Having grown up with older brothers and being raised to believe that she could achieve anything her brothers could, she had the courage she needed to deal with criticism and simply get on with the job. Another challenge came in the form of her salary. When she asked for advice regarding how much she would ask for, she was advised by a PGA exec to ask for less. Fortunately, she chose not to take his advice!

Marriott, who was performing consultancy work for the Arizona State University women's team and was director of instruction at Karsten Golf Course, was also inspired to try something new.

The name of their school. Vision54, which is located in Scottsdale, is based on one question: If pro players birdie every hole in their home course at some point in their preparation, why couldn't they manage to achieve this in one single read? If they shot 18-under on a par 72 course, then their score would be 54!

Their project managed to achieve immense success and was ranked as one of the top golf academies in the US by Golf Digest! One of the reasons is that Nilsson and Marriott are interested in more than simply "improving a swing." They don't just teach their students *what* to do, but also *how* to do it. Specifically, they hone in on how players can commit to making key decisions, manage the many variables that can occur during a game, and manage their stress levels and emotions.

Their aim is to tap into the innate joy of playing golf, something that every player can do (AZ Golf Homes, n.d.). The duo's list of clients is vast and includes Annika Sorenstam, Ai Miyazato, Ariya Jutanugarn, Kevin Streelman, and Russell Knox.

17

THE MAN WHO OUTPLAYED BING CROSBY WITH A BASEBALL BAT

"There was a touch of unreality, a mystery about him from the start... He wasn't part of the perpetual stream of tap-dancers and cowboys and lounge singers hoping to find celluloid stardom on the back lots of the movie studios. He was a golfer. He wanted to play golf."

— LEIGH MONTVILLE

John Montague ("Monty" to his friends) was a golfer who seemingly appeared out of nowhere, playing his first rounds on public courses in Hollywood, California in the 1930s. Nobody knew where he came from, or why he played so well—let alone how he made a living!

He drove fancy cars, dressed in designer clothing, and set new course records various times within a few months. He was known for his long drive and birdie putts, and was said to have the unique ability to sculpt shots around trees and evade impossible obstacles, or blast a ball out of a sandpit to the perfect spot. He was no less than a wonder on the greens.

Monty was the champ of the Lakeside Golf Club—which was so close to three major movie studios, that many of its members belonged to the glitterati. It was so near to Universal Studios that players could hear tigers, elephants, and lions while they walked along the fairways and greens. Typical faces you might see on the course included Tarzan himself (Johnny Weissmuller), Douglas Fairbanks, W.C. Fields, and Howard Hughes.

Monty was known for his unusual strength. He once pulled a drowning woman out of a dam and lifted acclaimed comedian, Oliver Hardy (who weighed 300 pounds) onto a bar using just one hand. Now this wasn't an ordinary bar! It was a narrow one that felt like a tightrope to Hardy. If he fell the wrong way, he could be injured, and even if he did manage to find his balance on top, he would eventually fall! Monty would make Hardy sweat for a few seconds before finally offering a hand and helping him down. He did this every time Hardy would arrive at the Lakeside grillroom—so much so that the comedian used to poke his head into the door and ask "Is

Monty here?" before daring to step in from a drink. No matter how often Monty performed this stunt, it still drew laughs and was always appreciated for the amazing feat of strength that it was!

He also stuffed the famous character actor, George Bancroft, into a Lakeside locker room, apparently because he heard Bancroft curse in front of the women at the club! Another version has it that the two were simply engaged in a contest of strength, and Monty decided to stuff an upside-down Bancroft into a locker and shut the door! Bancroft apparently had to beg for someone to release him.

Monty was also fond of moving cars with his bare hands. Golfer, Gene Andrews, recalls that one day, while they were playing golf, there was a 1928 Buick parked out in front. Montague said he'd move it to get it out of the way. True to his word, he lifted the entire vehicle and placed it a full three feet from where it had been parked (Montville 2008).

Johnny Weissmuller, who himself was famed for his strength, recalls that Monty's power was quite simply out of this world. They were out one night and for some reason, words were crossed with the driver of another car. It had seemingly been Monty's fault, as the right of way belonged to the other driver. Weissmuller says that the driver walked up and began cursing at them. Without a word, Monty went up to the other car, lifted it off the ground, and let it drop, "One of the lights fell off and Monty just walked back to the guy and said, 'What did you say?' The smart guy almost fainted as we drove off." (Montville 2008).

There are a hundred funny stories about Monty, but one that remains in golfers' collective memory is the time he won a special match against Bing Crosby. The crooner was a good golfer who lived on Toluca Lake and sometimes played 36 holes in a single day. One day, while playing with (and losing to) Monty, he bemoaned his misfortune, blaming his defeat on a bad bounce, a bad lie, and other trivialities. Monty disagreed. He claimed that a mere turn of luck would not have made any difference to the results. He put his money where his mouth was, challenging Crosby to a one-hole rematch. Monty offered to use a baseball bat, shovel, and rake instead of golf clubs. He was confident, he said, that he would still beat Crosby —and he was right!

He hit a ball 350 yards into a sand trap with the baseball bat, then shoveled the ball to within eight feet of the hole. Finally, he got down on all fours and made the putt for the birdie using the rake's handle. This beat Crosby's par 4, which was executed using a drive, chip, and two putts, all with his usual clubs.

It was enough to convince Crosby, who returned to the bar for more festivities. The story, however, ran like fire through Hollywood and was exaggerated by some, who claimed the match took place over 18 holes! Montague had already developed a reputation for being uniquely strong, humorous, and brash, but from this point onwards, he was known as "the man who beat Bing Crosby using a baseball bat, a shovel, and a rake."

18

THERE'S SOMETHING FISHY GOING ON!

"Take a bite out of life, live fiercely, and stay sharp!"

— AN ANONYMOUS SHARK

You would think that a golf course with sharks in its lake would be avoided by golfers, but in fact, people come from all over the world to see the bull sharks at the 15th hole of Australia's Carbrook Golf Club.

You may wonder how a school of sharks managed to make their way to this well-reputed club, which is one of the few members-owned clubs established in Queensland, Australia, in the past 60 years. The par 71 golf course is of championship standard. It has 18 holes and measures around 6,107 meters. It boasts stunning fairways, quick greens, an aesthetically pleasing layout, and between six and twelve bull sharks in its bordering lake!

The first question that may pop into your mind is—how on Earth did they get there? The answer is simple: a river flood swept these predators into a nearby lake in the 1990s. Over the next few years, golfers claimed that they could see them, but this remained a bit of an urban myth. Then, in the early 2000s, someone caught the sharks on camera.

Since their arrival, the jagged-toothed "invaders" have grown to humongous sizes and bred consistently, so there is never a shortage of them. This means that if you do score an invitation to the club, it's likely that you will manage to capture a few pics of the sharks enjoying a swim.

You may wonder if bull sharks are harmless. Actually, they're not! They are considered to be one of the most dangerous species due to their aggressive behavior and fondness for shallow waters. They are known for their large size, with adults reaching a length of up to 11 feet and weighing up to 500 pounds. Their favorite prey are fish and squid, but they have been known to attack humans whenever they feel threatened, or when they confuse human beings for prey.

They have been witnessed hunting in groups and attacking their victims in a coordinated fashion. The International Shark Attack File reports that there have been 27 unprovoked bull shark attacks on humans alone since 220. They also happen to be one of the few shark species that can tolerate fresh water (American Oceans, n.d.).

Thankfully, none of the golfers at Carbrook have been harmed. In fact, some dare to feed the sharks, leading to the rather hair-raising image of sharks rising from the water. If it's all feeling a bit too similar to Jaws for your liking, then give this club a miss!

When it comes to golf, sharks may not be the only animals you have to watch out for. One Florida golfer survived an alligator attack in 2017 that might have ended his life, had he not been a quick thinker and used his putter to defend himself.

The golfer's name was Tony Aarts, and he was enjoying an otherwise peaceful game at Magnolia Landing Golf & Country Club in North Fort Myers, Florida (Chiari 2017). Aarts was grabbed by the gator swiftly, and found himself in the water up to his waist. He recalls, "And I'm thinking I'm getting deeper and deeper, and I thought you're not gonna get me." He swung at the thick-skinned predator a few times until the gator finally relented and let go of his foot. He managed to crawl his way out of the water and the gator was captured by the Florida Fish and Wildlife Conservation Commission.

In July 2023, another alligator attack occurred while a 79-year-old Florida man was walking at the Forest Glen and

Golf Course community at 5 am. The predator was a six-foot-nine-inch female who clearly thought she had found some breakfast! Luckily, the man had his phone on him and was able to call emergency services and his wounds were attended to speedily. "Go figure. Out for a walk to stay healthy," he joked. The sheriff's office warns local residents to steer clear of bodies of water and landscapes where alligators might be resting. Timing is also key. Alligators are most active between dusk and dawn, so it's best to avoid walks during this time (Riess 2023).

Florida is home to some 1.3 million alligators across its 67 counties. It boasts around 6.7 million wetland habitats. However, these reptiles are even more common in Louisiana, which houses two million gators thanks to its warm climate and swampland. Despite the impressive numbers, only one fatal attack has occurred in Louisiana since 1174.

If the idea of playing amidst wildlife thrills you, one course to watch out for is Kiawah Island Golf Resort in South Carolina, which has hosted a string of prestigious championships, including the Ryder Cup and PGA Championship. It also has a myriad of wildlife, including dolphins, bobcats, turtles, and alligators. Some can be found swimming in the water hazards, while others prefer basking in the sun on the greens. The reptiles at this club seem to be far more docile, however, with resort official, Bryan Hunter, telling CNN the only rules are not to bother or feed the animals. Anyone who bothers them receives a $2,000 fine. Feeding is prohibited because it is an indirect way of training alligators to associate human beings with food (Bantock 2022).

Many other golf courses across the globe support birds and other beautiful wildlife. For instance, in the UK, Sustainable Golf is working to actively support two of its fastest-declining bird species (willow tilts and turtle-doves). Many of this group's projects involve connecting golf courses to existing habitats. Other birds that benefit from this type of initiative are skylarks, curlews, cuckoos, swifts, and starlings. Golf courses can provide a safe habitat for these species, both during their breeding seasons and when they are simply passing through.

Without a doubt, one of the most appealing courses when it comes to wildlife is the Baobab Course at Vipingo Ridge, in Kenya (the only PGA-accredit golf course in this country). The course has a vital connection with the animal kingdom and players frequently enjoy visits from deer, giraffes, and alligators. Many animals arrive as rescues, and they are free to roam the entirety of the course, which is peppered with indigenous trees for the four-footed guests!

19

GRIP IT AND RIP IT

"Winners see what they want. Losers see what they don't want. Don't let the game eat you; you eat the game."

— MOE NORMAN

Canadian golfer, Moe Norman, has been touted as golf's most misunderstood genius and is sometimes referred to as "the Rain Man of Golf" because, like Dustin Hoffman's character in the film Rain Man, he was an autistic savant.

Among professionals, he is a mythical figure who represented what true sporting giftedness looks like. Paul Azinger, who was a college player when he first saw Moe play, said, "He started ripping these drivers right off the ground at the 250-yard marker, and he never hit one more than 10 yards to either side of it, and he hit at least 50." Azinger also told Tim O'Connor (author of Moe's life story, The Feeling of Greatness) that Moe could predict the exact number of times that his ball would bounce after he had hit it. And he never failed! (Owen 2020).

Moe didn't fit into the traditional mold of the average pro golfer. He spoke in staccato bursts, repeated what he said twice, and wore eccentric clothing. He referred to himself as "the best ball striker" in the history of the sport, and his peers had no choice but to agree, for he was incredibly accurate. Lee Trevino, for instance, thought Moe was one of the best golfers who ever lived, alongside Byron Nelson and Ben Hogan. This was the case despite the fact that he only made a showing in the Masters twice.

He was best known for his single-plane swing and his unusually straight stroke. He used to hit hundreds of 250-yard drives, one after the other, and all of them would straight ahead. He was compared to Iron Byron, the driving machine that was developed to put zero spin on a ball. His tee shots landed on top of each other in consecutive fashion and filled greens with dozens of five-iron shots. To this day, some schools teach Mo's famous single-plane golf swing. It simplifies the golf swing and aims to teach golfers to shoot straight. It is considered by some to be the easiest way to play, because you have fewer "moving parts" during the entire motion.

He was also known for his uncanny ability to shoot through trees and successfully avoid obstacles—but only if he could see the holes.

Moe was a fast player. At the 1956 Masters, a player asked him why he took such little time to line up his shots. "Why? Did they move the greens since yesterday?" he asked. By this stage, he had come up with his unique way of lining up shots flawlessly.

Despite his immense talent, Moe Norman never became a household name in his country. His "eccentric" personality, the fact that he didn't shine on PGA Tours as much as his contemporaries and his intense shyness may all have contributed to his relative obscurity. However, as Tim O'Connor states, Moe's star would undoubtedly have shone much brighter if he had been born in this era of greater diversity.

Without a doubt, Moe's story was fascinating from the start. As a child, he was an avid hockey player, but when he discovered golf and became a caddy, he realized he had found his passion. This fueled a bit of strife with his working-class family, who wondered why Moe was so fascinated by this "elite" sport. Their rejection of the thing he loved the most led to a distance that would last throughout his lifetime.

It was during his late teens and twenties that Moe began to concentrate on his swing. He was determined to achieve accuracy and reduce variability. His hit ensured that the club's shaft position was kept in place during impact. His stance was wide, his pose outstretched, and his hands aligned. While swinging, he achieved the perfect synchronization of his hips, hands, arms, and shoulders. Such was his determination that Moe apparently stayed on the course for hours, playing until his hands bled. As his fame grew, he began holding clinics in which he shared his technique with others. His aim was never to win trophies, but rather to achieve something that went beyond himself. He aspired to own a "feeling of greatness." (Morse 2021).

Many fans wonder what made Moe so unique. O'Connor has interviewed neuroscientists, who believe that his personality might have resulted from a frontal lobe injury, sustained when he was just five years of age. He was out sledding when a truck wheel ran over one side of his head. He was dragged for a long distance, and remembered the sensation of a tire rolling over one side of his face. This occurred during the era of the Great Depression and his parents, who were struggling financially, didn't take him to the hospital because he didn't have any broken bones. However, his mother worried that the accident had caused her son's personality to completely change. Moe became lonely and found refuge in the sport he loved.

Moe was different, and he was made to suffer for it. While competing in the US Tour, he decided to pull out. Some players had taken offense at Moe hitting the ball off the big tee and had bullied him about the way he dressed. It stopped him from enjoying the game and he decided he would never play on that Tour again.

Moe's life wasn't all about challenges. He also had some lucky greats. In the early 1980s, Moe met Jack Kuykendall —a successful Chicago businessman with dreams of going pro. Kuykendall was a physics major in college, and he devised a special swing based on physics principles. One day, he came across a video of Moe playing and was flabbergasted. Moe's swing was identical to the system he had devised! Kuykendall deemed Moe's swing to be perfect, since it produced maximum force with minimal effort. He contacted Moe and the businessman's company, Natural Golf, conducted several dozen clinics per year alongside Moe, paying him a generous sum. This alliance led to a collaboration with Titleist, a company that offered to pay him $5,000 for the rest of his life. (Owen 2020).

Moe passed away in 2004, at the age of 75. He will justly be remembered as a true golf pioneer and one of golf's most misunderstood players.

THE DAY DISTRACTION LOST THE VICTOR THE GREEN JACKET

"Golf is like love. One day you think you are too old and the next day you want to do it again."

— ROBERTO DE VICENZO

The US Masters, one of golf's four major tournaments, is universally known as the most prestigious tournament in the world by pro and amateur players alike. Winning the Masters is considered an arduous task, and it is no wonder that two of the greatest golfers of all time have a record number of wins at Augusta: Jack Nicklaus and Tiger Woods.

There's an old saying that you don't go to August to find your game. You had better have it with you when you get there! It is true today, and it was true when Roberto De

Vicenzo made what was arguably the biggest mistake of his life, giving the green jacket away because of a silly mistake!

The occasion was the 1968 Masters and De Vicenzo—an Argentinean star who won a whopping 215 titles, including the World Cups of 1953, 1962, and 1970—made a move that would go down in Masters history. For he made a very silly and costly mistake. He signed an incorrect scorecard after the 72nd hole of the Masters, knocking himself out of a playoff with Bob Goalby (Andalucia Golf, n.d.).

Goalby shot a final-round of 66, but De Vicenzo had set the course ablaze with a 65. Unfortunately for De Vicenzo, his playing partner for the final round, Tommy Aaron, had mistakenly marked a 4 on De Vicenzo's scorecard at the 17th hole instead of the birdie three he had actually shot. The final leaderboard saw Bob Goalby with 277 strokes and De Vicenzo with 278. After the round, De Vicenzo failed to notice the error and he signed the scorecard.

Within minutes of the fateful error, Masters and Augusta officials gathered together in secret to discuss the situation. The rules stated that a player who signed a card with a higher score had to stand by that score, while a player who signed a card with a lower score was automatically disqualified. Still, they sought the advice of one of golf's most famous players, Bobby Jones—who was ill and taking some rest in a fairway cottage. Jones' opinion was that the rules could not be bent, regardless of the circumstances. As such, The officials returned to the clubhouse and informed De Vicenzo of the unfortunate decision.

Luckily, De Vicenzo took it well! He jokingly blamed Goalby, saying he had laid the pressure on so thick that it caused him to lose his mind. He said that he had played the best golf of his life, but made two crucial mistakes. The first was a hook on the last hole and the second was signing the wrong scorecard. "I feel sorry for me. I think I go get a drink and go home," he said. Then he uttered the words that would be remembered and used by many a golfer in years to come: "I was just a stupid." His words were boldly printed beneath his image on the cover of Sports Illustrated (Tosches 1989).

De Vicenzo never blamed Aaron, who ironically had been a mathematics major at the University of Florida. Aaron chalked the error up to nerves. When De Vicenzo hit a sixth birdie on hole 17, Aaron recalled, the crowd went wild. But an even louder cheer came from the 15th hole, where Goalby had landed an eagle to pull even at 12 under. He recalls that the moment was tense—so much so that he forgot to jot Roberto's score down before he left the green.

Aaron states that at the 18th tee, the one thing on his mind was that De Vicenzo had a chance of winning if he achieved par. Yet he made a bogey five, which left him distraught. As they left the green and sat down to score, Aaron was thinking that it was a real shame that De Vicenzo no longer stood a chance. Aaron then wrote his friend's last two scores—bogey 5 at the last and par 4 at 17 —a 4 that was sadly incorrect. He then passed De Vicenzo the card for him to sign. But the latter was still in shock over the finish, and he sat there, holding his head in his hands.

Just then, someone came up to the duo and told De Vicenzo he was needed in the press room. As a result, he quickly signed the card without checking it. It was only when Aaron gazed up at the big scoreboard that he realized something was wrong. They had De Vicenzo for 65, one less than Aaron. It suddenly hit him. He had mistakenly given him a 4 on the 17th. When he told De Vicenzo, the latter suggested changing the card. But it was impossible, answered Aaron, since this would amount to breaking the rules.

Despite Goalby's bogey on the 17th, he was declared the winner. But for Aaron, nobody won that day. De Vicenzo's loss was the most painful of all, but Goalby also received severe criticism and a pile of hate mail, and Aaron himself was widely criticized for his error. Luckily, he was backed by Jack Nicklaus, who declared the responsibility to lie with De Vicenzo (Links Magazine, n.d.).

Aaron claims he fought many demons over the years because of this fateful day. Five years later, he won the green jacket himself. Funnily enough, in the final round that year, his playing companion, Johnny Miller, recorded a wrong score for him on one hole. But he did the one thing De Vicenzo had failed to do: he checked his card and found the error!

21

THE CONCESSION

"I don't think you would have missed that putt, but in these circumstances, I would never give you the opportunity."

— JACK NICKLAUS

G reat rivalries don't have to be built on hatred and indeed, when they lean on mutual respect and admiration, two "enemies" can bring out the best in each other. This is exactly what occurred at the 1969 Ryder Cup, when Jack Nicklaus did something no player had done before—concede a putt to his foe!

It was the final day of the cup, and the overall score between the US and Team Great Britain was tied. The decisive match was to be played by Jack Nicklaus (representing the US) and Tony Jacklin (who had won the

British Open that year). The Cup had been marred by tense confrontations between the teams, and shredded nerves and frayed tempers had manifested themselves throughout the competition (Dimeglio, n.d.).

On the 18th hole, both Nicklaus and Jacklin had some putts to sink before claiming victory. 31 matches had been completed and the score stood at 15 ½-15 ½. Both Nicklaus and Jacklin were on the green in 2 at the par -4 hole. Jacklin's putt was about two feet short, while Nicklaus' ball landed five feet from the hole. Nicklaus scored a birdie, virtually guaranteeing the victory. However, instead of claiming victory outright, he conceded Jacklin's short putt, resulting in a tied match and allowing the Ryder Cup to end in a draw.

The gesture shocked the public at that precise instance, but it has come to be hailed as one of the most powerful acts of sportsmanship and goodwill, as it stopped Jacklin from losing a definitive match. The result was a tie for both teams, and both raised the Ryder Cup trophy.

Nicklaus subsequently explained what was running through his head at the time: "I very quickly thought about Tony Jacklin and what he had meant to British golf. Here he was, the Open champion, the new hero,..." Jack was worried that if Tony missed, he would be grilled in the press and lambasted by the public. The thoughts raced through his head in quick succession and suddenly, one idea felt right: he would not give Jacklin the chance to miss the shot. "I think we walk off of here, shake hands and have a better relationship between the two golfing organizations is the right way to do it." (Hardisty 2018).

When Nicklaus took his ball from the hole, he also picked up Jacklin's marker and the pair walked off the greens together, arm in arm. Nicklaus and his teammates took the Cup back to the US, but the Golden Bear's generosity sparked a new era of camaraderie that had simply not existed before.

Nicklaus' generous act may be the most memorable of its kind in golf, but it wasn't the first. At the 1920 British Amateur, Bobby Jones called a one-stroke penalty on himself when he accidentally moved the ball in the rough. There were no referees to call it a foul, or officials to slap him with a penalty. His playing companion, Walter Hagen, hadn't spotted the infraction. Nor had the spectators or even Jones' own caddie! The tournament was completed as usual, but it was only when the match was over that it was revealed that Jones had scored himself a penalty. This despite the fact that the fact that the ball had moved a little had not helped him, Nor was it a big violation to be concerned about. His honesty cost him the hole, but he managed to win the match anyway! When he was lauded afterward for his sportsmanship, Jones answered, "You might as well praise me for not robbing banks!" (Harrig 2007).

The 1996 event is remembered for something else: the alleged unsportsmanlike behavior of the US team on the 17th green. Justin Leonard had sunk a 45-foot putt that was decisive for their victory. At the time, José María Olazábal was waiting at the 17th to hit a 30-foot putt for the tie. It was a challenge, but Olazábal had sunk similar putts before. "That kind of behavior is not anything a golfer expects. It was sad to see . . . an ugly picture," Olazábal said (Boswell 1999).

At the 1999 Ryder Cup, another brilliant concession took place when six-time European leader, Colin Montgomerie, and two-time US Open champion, arrived at the 18th green at The Country Club in Brookline, Massachusetts. Everything boiled down to one last, tricky putt that Montgomerie had to sink. The win was his if he landed it. But if he missed, Stewart would tie against him and the US team's final margin would be a more decisive 15-13, not 14 ½-13 ½. Stewart instructed Montgomerie to pick up the ball, thus ensuring his own defeat. Stewart recalls, "As (Montgomerie) was getting ready to putt, I said to my caddie, 'He doesn't deserve to have to make this putt. I'm not going to make him do it. I'm not going to put him through that [if he misses]."

In fact, as far back as 1975, a concession was made during the playoff round of the 1975 British Open. Tom Watson was leading by two shots and on the 17th, his rival, Jack Newton, missed a short putt. Watson thought it would be cruel if Newton putted out and missed, so he conceded the hole and the match to Newton.

There were other golfers whose kindness and generosity were similar to Nicklaus'. At the 1996 Masters, in a competitive final round between Greg Norman and Nick Faldo, the latter praised "The Shark," encouraging him even when tensions were high. Most recently, at the 2016 Ryder Cup, Rory McIlroy and Patrick Reed took part in a memorable battle. Despite their rivalry, they exchanged friendly banter and fist pumps, celebrating the joy of golf despite all that was at stake!

22

GET A NEW DREAM

"If there is something you really want to do—no matter how impossible it may seem—with enough hard work and perseverance, you can do it."

— DENNIS WALTERS

Dennis Walters is a World Hall of Fame golfer who, in his own words, has been "touring" for over four decades. He has a whopping 3,000 events under his belt and has shone in some of the world's best courses, including Pebble Beach and St Andrews. He has also touched the lives of tens of thousands of people across the globe owing to his fighting spirit and mental toughness.

Dennis began playing when he was just eight years old. He discovered golf all on his own. He was walking to school one day, and he knew there was a golf course nearby. He walked through the woods to find it, and became fascinated by what he saw—a deer, squirrels, and a myriad of birds. He popped out of the woods and arrived on the 18th tee. He was fascinated when the golfer who was there swung his club and sent the ball through the air around 250 yards. He remembered thinking that it was a lot further than he could throw a baseball! That day, he went home and told his father, who offered his son to take him to play one day. His father took him to a semi-private course and gave him a golf club that he treasures to this day. Four years after starting, he knew that he wanted to dedicate his life to golf.

Dennis played against championship players like Lanny Wadkins, Andy North, and Craig Stadler, winning numerous medals as a college player and top amateur and missing out by two strokes to earn the right to play the Masters. His next step was to play the South African Tour, which was favored by aspiring players from Europe and the US. The weather was ideal, the courses top-notch, and the competition tough. After months in Johannesburg, he was ready to attend the US Tour qualifying school.

What he never suspected was that he would become involved in a freak accident that would paralyze him from the waist down. He was looking for his coach, who was out on the golf course, so he got into a buggy to get to him faster. As he took a curve on the path, the three-wheeled buggy turned over, throwing him onto the ground. He felt no pain at all and didn't have a scratch on him. However, when he tried to get up, he was surprised to find he could not move his legs. He was found by a group who called an ambulance. The hospital would be his home for the following four months (EDGA Golf, n.d.).

Dennis was distraught. His dream of completing his training for the Tour was dashed and he began to worry that he would never again regain feeling in his legs. His fears were confirmed when the doctor told him he would never walk again. Dennis recalls wondering why this had happened to him and why it occurred at this precise moment in his life.

One day, while Dennis and his father were watching his friends play golf on TV, Dennis began to weep. His father, a former military man with a deep and abiding love for his son, suggested that they go out and play a few balls. Before long, Dennis was on his chair at the local golf course with a Byron Nelson three-wood in his hand. He discovered challenges he had never faced before. For instance, his legs were in the way of his swing! His father, Bucky, had a great idea! He went back home and brought a cushion that made Dennis sit up taller. Now he had more room to swing. His father also secured his son to the chair with a belt. Eventually, Dennis was hitting so hard that the chair would tip. Bucky went home once again with a rope, which he used to secure the chair to a tree. Finally, Dennis was free to hit with all his might... and that is exactly what he did!

After a few weeks, he received an invitation to visit Crystal Lago Golf Club in Florida. There, he met Alex Ternyei, a semi-retired pro who used to make hickory clubs and taught the old-fashioned way, believing that authentic power came from the arms and hands more than the legs. Dennis knew that Alex would make the perfect teacher, precisely because of his philosophy. Every day, Walters would beat balls on the range at the club, with Ternyei teeing up his shots for him.

However, one day while at the clubhouse, Dennis, who was sitting on a stool, expressed that he was tired of just hitting balls. Alex looked at him and said, "When you wake up tomorrow, this swivel stool will be on a golf cart." (Rosaforte 1995). The following day, Walters was out playing golf. He used the swivel seat to hit shots from the cart, then walked to the putt on crutches and made one-handed putts. Just eight months after his doctors had told him he would never play again, he proved them all wrong.

He didn't just play golf, he earned a living off it. Learning trick shots and lengthening the shafts of his clubs to improve his precision. He performed a plethora of shows with eight "trick shots" that wowed his audience. In 1979, he appeared on the famed TV show, *That's Incredible!*, hitting balls out of the host's mouth while wearing a blindfold. He made his appearances on many tours, including the PGA and the LPGA.

He now earns a high, six-figure salary and has sponsors the likes of Yamaha and Cobra. The National Golf Foundation has honored him with the Graffis Award, for his outstanding contributions to the game. In 1978, he won the Ben Hogan Award for his courageous recovery.

Today, he is able to break par for nine holes from the front tees of his local club. He says that although he never got to do all he wanted, he still got the chance for his shots to mean something. Tiger Woods has said that Dennis "has inspired so many people." Gary Player, meanwhile, stated, "There is always light at the end of the tunnel. I just love this guy so much." Perhaps the most inspirational words, however, are Dennis' own: "Never let anyone tell you that your dream is impossible. And if your dream doesn't work out, that's okay. Get a new dream!" (Get a New Dream, n.d.).

23

FROM RAGS TO RICHES

"Every golf shot I hit, I thought about how much I wanted to eat."

— CHI CHI RODRIGUEZ

Juan Antonio "Chi Chi" Rodriguez, is one of golf's most charismatic players, famous for his "sword dance" celebration for birdie putts and for this authentic rag-to-riches success story. Chi Chi, who at five-foot-seven is one of the smallest golfers of his time, is also one of the game's most brilliant shot makers. His nickname comes from Puerto Rican Hall-of-Famer, Chi Chi Flores. Although Flores wasn't the best baseball player that ever lived, Rodriguez admired him because he was such a fighter.

He was born into a low-income family in 1935 in Rio Piedras, Puerto Rico. His father worked as a cattle handler and laborer and pocketed just $18 a week. At the age of seven, Chi Chi was already employed as a water carrier on a sugar plantation, and anything he earned was given to his parents to help feed his family.

He carved his first golf club from a tree branch and began striking rocks or "balls" made of rolled-up tin cans. Chi Chi was a great all-round athlete, and was known for his talent at boxing and baseball. At the age of eight, he started working as a caddie, attracted by the relatively large pay compared to what he earned on the plantation. Between shifts, he would sneak onto the golf course to practice. He said he envisioned a career in golf since his youth, and grew determined to pursue this profession to escape from a life of hunger.

By the age of 16, he was setting course records. At 17, he came in second at the Puerto Rico Open (Kelley 2019). He then enlisted in the army, working for two years before working at the Dorado Beach Resort. Even during his stint in the military, he never abandoned golf, enjoying games whenever he had free time. There, he chanced upon a PGA Tour pro, Cooper. The latter took him under his wing and served as a mentor for Chi Chi. Soon after, the Puerto Rican legend received the financial backing of Laurence Rockefeller and played his first PGA Tour in 1960.

He became a fan favorite in no time, owing to his imaginative shot shaping, acclaimed ball-striking abilities, and his showmanship. When he wasn't sword dancing, he was performing his "toreador dance," or laying his hat over a hole to "stop the ball from escaping." He was so well-loved by the public that he became a star. Such was his influence that his likeness was used as the cover art of new wave band, Devo's first album, released in 1978.

His first PGA Tour victory was in 1963, at the Denver Open. The following year, he won twice and came in ninth on the money list. His most acclaimed win also happened in 1964, when he beat Arnold Palmer at the legendary Western Open by one stroke.

Chi Chi won eight times while playing the PGA Tour, and his final PGA victory was at the Tallahassee Open in 1975. Where he really shone was on the Champions Tour. He won three times in the first year of his participation and in 1987, he won seven times, nabbing the Senior PGA Championship. He had 14 Top 3 finishes that year and held the top spot on the money list. He won a total of 22 times on this tour, with his last win occurring in 1993.

Chi Chi was famed for his long drives, accuracy with the irons, and creativity, and his biggest challenge lay in putting. The player once claimed, "I've heard people say putting is 50 percent technique and 50 percent mental. I really believe it is 50 percent technique and 90 percent positive thinking. See, but that adds up to 140 percent, which is why nobody is 100 percent sure how to putt." (Kelley, 2019). It is often said that pound-for-pound Chi Chi is the longest hitter in the history of the game. He was also highly skilled at bunker plays.

"How did he manage to hit such long drives?" you may ask. The answer was—he honed his strength! "I was an average hitter, not very long, as a young man. So, I went to a gym in Puerto Rico," he says. There, the trainer was insecure about helping Rodriguez, since he was not specialized in golf. Chi Chi's answer was that you don't need to know how to box to train a boxer! He asked the trainer to watch him swing, and the trainer developed a three-day-a-week routine that concentrated on specific muscles. This, says Chi Chi, added a whopping 75 yards to his drive. He recalls the applause when he outdrove Jack Nicklaus, whom he called "a legend in his spare time." (Kaufman 2021).

Now that he is in his mid-80s, Chi Chi is still a keen observer of the golfing scene. He actively helps struggling golfers achieve their dreams. He founded The Chi Chi Rodriguez Youth Foundation in Clearwater, which helps at-risk youth in the classroom and includes golf as part of the lesson plan. Its mission is to help kids improve their academic performance, boost their self-esteem, and build character by using the golf course as a living classroom. For Chi Chi Rodriquez, it was where many of his most important life lessons were learned. "Everything I've ever had, I've shared," he once said, and his life history is testimony to this fact.

CONFIDENCE IS EVERYTHING

> *"There are plenty of naturally talented, better golfers out there,"* he said. *"I just think mentally I might be stronger. And I've got a lot of self-belief in what I know I can do."*

— IAN POULTER

Who, in your view, is the best type of golfer? Is it the player with the undeniable, raw talent that is visible from a very young age (as was the case with Tiger Woods) or rather, one who has worked to overcome their deficiencies through self-belief and sheer hard work?

Ian Poulter was of the latter variety; a golfing great who started his professional career with a 4 handicap, but who built an incredibly successful career and became a veritable icon of European Ryder Cup history.

He started as young as any other golfer of his standard. In fact, he was just four years of age when his father, who had a handicap of 1, gave him a cut-down 3-wood (Planet Sport, n.d.). He was unable to get a spot as a pro at a private golf club, so he found another way in: by working as an assistant pro and golf shop manager at Chesfield Downs Golf and Country Club. He did have access to the course, but there was one big problem: he had to pay a full green free every time he wanted to compete. His 4 handicap was largely the result of the fact that he wasn't able to get out and compete as often as he wanted to.

Luckily, he caught the eye of Lee Scarbrow—a renowned teacher who identified great talent in the then-17-year-old. Ian joined Scarbrow at Leighton Buzzard Golf Course as an Assistant Pro, teaching young players for just £1 per class. Scarbow worked for six years alongside Poulter, serving as both his boss and coach.

When speaking of his famous pupil, Scarbrow acknowledges that with Ian, the magic was more in his mentality rather than his technique. He recalls that even as a teen, Ian was convinced that he wanted to be a top-level golf pro: "He was always going to be a European Tour winner, a World Cup winner, and a Ryder Cup player. He never spoke to me about if, just when!" said Scarbrow.

The coach has also highlighted his pupil's intense focus and self-belief. The more pressure he felt, said the coach, the sharper his concentration became. What's more,

Poulter believed that the roll he put on the ball was supreme. Scarbrow has also spoken about the player's active imagination and ability to "see the line of his putts" in his mind's eye (Today's Golfer 2013).

Scarbow himself had a fascinating life. When he was in his 20s, he aspired to be a tour player, but both his lungs collapsed and his main goal was simply to breathe. During his recovery, he realized that he would not be able to compete professionally, but he knew that he still wanted to dedicate himself to golf. Therefore, he switched to coaching, and found that it was every bit as satisfying—if not more so, than actually playing it. He has stated, "What I love more than anything is watching lights switch on – someone getting what you want them to do; the thought that actually they can do this." (PGA 2022). And that didn't take long with Poulter, who never doubted himself for a second.

Poulter finally made it as a pro in the 1990s, and began picking up a string of victories—including an impressive win at the Italian Open, which led him to receive the European Tour's Sir Henry Cotton Rookie of the Year award. During his first four seasons, he showed his competitors what he was made of, defeating players the caliber of Sergio García at the 2004 Volvo Masters Andalucía. It was a sign of his ability to keep his calm under pressure and compete against the world's best.

The Majors have never been Poulter's thing, as he has almost (but not quite) emerged victorious at many—including the 2008 British Open. Poulter finished second after Irish champ Padraig Harrington, despite carding an enviable final round of 69. He finished tied third at the 2012 PGA and at the 2013 British Open. He has achieved eight top-ten finishes.

The World Golf Championships were another thing altogether for the Englishman. He boasts three PGA Tour Victories (the 2010 World Golf Championships-Accenture Match Play Championship, the 2012 World Golf Championships-HSBC Champions, and the 2018 Houston Open. He also has 12 international victories under his belt, including the 2011 Volvo World Match Play Championship in Europe and the JBWere Masters in Australia (PGA Tour Media Guide, n.d.).

Many would say that the place where Poulter really shone was at the Ryder Cup. He was a particularly brilliant matchplay performer, scoring four wins at the 2012 Ryder Cup and forming a major part of the Miracle at Medinah. He also won four points from five matches in a losing clause in 208, and three from four two years later. He has won 14 (and halved four) of his 22 matches and has blazed the trail in terms of his performance in the singles.

Poulter was almost as famous for his quirky dress sense as he was for his talent at golf! And there are family reasons for his love of fashion: his mother managed a branch of

UK women's clothing chain, Dorothy Perkins. Some of his most famous ensembles included trousers featuring the famous Claret Jug (the trophy that recognizes the Champion Golfer of the Year), which he wore at the 2005 and 2006 Open Championships.

He was famed for clashing with the greens thanks to his "loud" pants, which featured everything from checkered patterns to Union Jacks, polka dots, and other eye-catching designs. His shirts are equally loud and are sometimes made in shiny metallic fabrics. He also likes to occasionally play with unique shoe designs. He occasionally sports high-top shoes—a rarity considering that most golfers prefer the traditional low-cut style. And let's not forget his visors and flat caps, which add a touch of British flair to his creative looks!

A FAMOUS FEUD

> *"I look into eyes, shake their hand, pat their back, and wish them luck, but I am thinking, I am going to bury you."*
>
> — SEVE BALLESTEROS

S eve Ballesteros was unforgettable, not only for his exceptional teamwork and sportsmanship but also for his honest, no-BS personality. The man was well-loved, as you will recall from our chapter on The Miracle at Medinah. However, he saw no problem in telling it like it was, especially when someone tempted his patience—as Paul Azinger did in 1989.

The animosity began when Seve and Paul first came face-to-face at The Belfry. Seve already had five major titles to his name, while Paul's biggest achievement was finishing runner-up to Nick Faldo at the 1987 British Open. Both were at the top of the singles list, and the pressure started to get to them. Seve indicated that he would be changing his damaged ball on the green and Azinger demanded to see evidence of the damage. Upon closer inspection, he declared that the ball was playable, and insisted that Seve not be permitted to make the change. Seve struck back later, by asking Paul if he had dropped his ball properly after hitting it into a water hazard on the 18th hole. Azinger won the match 1-up but Europe kept the trophy thanks to the 14-14 tie (RTL Today, 223).

Two years later, the players locked horns again at Kiawah Island. Azinger and Chip Beck were challenging Ballesteros and Jose Maria Olazábal (the Spanish Armada). The rules of the tournament stipulate that all players have to use the same type of ball they start with when hitting off driving holes. Beck, who was first off the tee at the odd-numbered holes, should have used his 90-compression ball when driving at the seventh. But the pair decided they might achieve a better score Beck used Azinger's 100-compression ball.

"Why does compression matter so much?" you may ask. Essentially, all golf balls are assigned a compression rating (from 40 to 100). The lower the rating, the more easily it compresses when struck by a club. The rating is closely related to swing speed. Golfers with slow swing speeds tend to choose lower-compression balls because they compress easily and produce greater distance. Those with fast swings, meanwhile, go for higher compression balls, in order to control the spin and maintain distance. The compression of a ball can make a big difference to the outcome, affecting everything from the feel of the ball at impact to the trajectory and flight characteristics of the ball.

Ballesteros took his time and objected to the Americans' play of the seventh when it was too late to claim the hole. Azinger and Beck crumbled under the pressure, losing hole after hole. The Spaniards took five out of eight holes to win the match 2 and 1.

Azinger recalls that he was furious when Ballesteros called an official on the 10th tee, as their intention had never been to deceive their opponents. A heated discussion took place with the official in front of a large crowd and it was filmed for all the world to see. After the match, Ballesteros told the press that Azinger had changed the ball not once, but three times! "At first he denied it completely, then when he realized they could not lose the hole he changed his statement," he said. Azinger also had a few things to say. He sarcastically called Ballesteros "the king of gamesmanship" and accused him of coughing while the Americans were playing. Ballesteros completely denied trying to distract other players. His teammate, Olazábal, recognized that both he and Ballesteros had been ill that week, but that they never coughed while other players were hitting shots.

Just a year before this feud, Azinger had made another enemy: Nick Faldo. During the 1987 British Open at Muirfield, Faldo beat Azinger by a single stroke. One year later, in 1989, Azinger again ruffled Faldo's feathers by accusing him of standing too close to his partner, Chick Beck, as the latter was lining up a putt. "I'll read my partner's putt, if you don't mind," Azinger snapped.

When they met again six years later at the Belfry in 1993, sparks once again flew. The players were head-to-head on the final singles match on Sunday and both were giving an impeccable performance. Faldo made a hole-in-one at the 14th to go on up. Azinger birdied the next to level him. By the time they reached the 18th hole, the US had won the Cup. Azinger was facing a six-foot putt to half the match and he expected a concession from Faldo. He didn't get it! It would have been the gracious thing to do, said Azinger, but he holed it for a half anyway.

In 2008, the two seemingly reconciled, and many thought they would be a cheerful, dynamic duo henceforward. However, Azinger gave an interview in which he stated that most other players "hated" Faldo. He said that although Faldo had tried to redefine himself, some people simply didn't buy it. "But if you're going to be a prick and everyone hates you, why do you think that just because you're trying to be cute and funny on air now, that the same people are all going to start to like you?" he said. (Donegan, 2008).

What about Azinger and Ballesteros, did they ever make peace? Indeed, they did! In fact, when Azinger was diagnosed with a serious illness (he developed lymphoma in his right shoulder blade), Ballesteros was one of the first people to call him. "It was impossible not to love Seve, except for one week every two years." In 2004, both were inducted into the World Golf Hall of Fame and they shared the stage to address the audience. Ballesteros praised Azinger as a fantastic player and fierce competitor, and said he was proud to have been his rival. Azinger echoed Ballesteros' generosity, calling him one of the greatest players of all time. When Ballesteros passed away in 2011, Azinger called him a true friend and an unforgettable golfing legend.

ARNOLD PALMER, A GOLFING LEGEND

"Golf is deceptively simple and endlessly complicated; it satisfies the soul and frustrates the intellect. It is at the same time rewarding and maddening—and it is without a doubt the greatest game mankind has ever invented."

— ARNOLD PALMER

There are many good reasons why Arnold Palmer is called "The King." He shone brightly in the 1950s and 1960s, dazzling audiences with his unorthodox swing and his aggressive approach to the game. He was the first player to win the Masters four times and the first to take home $1 million in prize money. He played for over 50 years, reigning supreme in 92 tournaments, 62 of which were on the PGA. His following was huge and loyal, and they referred to themselves as "Arnie's Army."

Arnold's inimitable rise to fame began when he was just four and he began swinging his first set of clubs, which had been cut down for him by his father, Milfred (who worked at Latrobe Country Club for over 50 years as a golf pro and course superintendent). It didn't take other players long to recognize his formidable talent, as he was beating caddies who were far older than he was. At the age of 11, he became a caddie himself and undertook a host of different jobs at the club.

He played golf in high school and during his college years, and won his first of five West Penn Amateur Championships when he was just 17. While studying at Wake Forest University, he was deeply affected by the death in a car crash of his good friend, Bud Worsham. He ditched college and began a three-year stint in the Coast Guard. While he was stationed in Cleveland, his interest in golf was rekindled. He began playing amateur golf after discharge from the service and returned to Wake Forest. In 1954, he won the US Amateur, and it was clear that he was made for this sport. He turned pro four months later.

Arnold's peak period was between 1960 and 1963, when he won 29 titles and earned close to $400,00 at a time in which prizes were far smaller than they are today. He was the top money winner during this time and represented the US twice in the Ryder Cup, captaining his team and leading them to victory in 1963.

Arnold was known for much more than his brilliance on the greens. He was a sharp businessman, and the President of Arnold Palmer Enterprises, which governed much of his global commercial activities. He also owned a car dealership and was involved in the automobile and aviation industries for many years. In 1999, he was recognized for his contributions to the aviation industry when the Westmoreland County Airport at Latrobe was renamed the Arnold Palmer Regional Airport. As if all this wasn't enough to keep him busy, he was also President and sole owner of Latrobe Country Club, and President and main owner of the Bay Hill Club and Lodge in Orlando, Florida. He additionally served on the board of directors of Laurel Valley Golf Club in PA.

Palmer was well-loved by the media and dabbled in it himself, serving as a consultant to the Golf Channel in Orlando. He lent his expertise and talent for design to a myriad of golf courses, putting his stamp on 300 of the best courses across the globe.

He won a string of awards, including a Presidential Medal of Freedom in 2004 and a Congressional Gold Medal. After his stellar 1960 performances, he won the Hickok Professional Athlete of the Year and Sports Illustrated's Sportsman of the Year trophies. He was a charter member of the World Golf Hall of Fame, chairman of the USGA Members Program, and honorary national chairman of the March of Dimes Birth Defects Foundation for two decades.

In the 1980s, Arnold took part in a major fundraising effort to build the Arnold Palmer Hospital for Children and Women, as well as the Arnold Palmer Medical Center in Orlando. He additionally served on the board of the Latrobe Area Hospital, for which he held an annual golf fundraising event.

Palmer's biographer, James Dodson, hit the nail on the head when he described what made Arnold so special: "He represented everything that is great about golf. The friendship, the fellowship, the laughter, the impossibility of golf, the sudden rapture moment that brings you back, a moment that you never forget, that's Arnold Palmer in spades. He's the defining figure in golf." (Schupak, 2016).

Fun Facts About Arnold Palmer

- He is credited with bringing golf to the mainstream and making it popular with people outside the world of exclusive country clubs.
- He is fifth on the Tour's all-time victory list, after Sam Snead, Tiger Woods, Jack Nicklaus, and Ben Hogan.
- These are the seven major championships he won:

  - U.S. Open: 1960
  - The Open Championship: 1961, 1962
  - Masters Tournament: 1958, 1960, 1962, 1964

- Palmer's caddie for all his Masters wins was Nathaniel "Iron Man" Avery. Back then, Augusta required all players to use the Club's own caddies.
- Palmer played on six Ryder Cup teams: in 1961, 1963, 1965, 1967, 1971, and 1973.
- Palmer is mentioned in the James Bond film, Goldfinger. In one scene, Bond's caddie states, "If that's [Goldfinger's] original ball, I'm Arnold Palmer."
- Palmer was also an avid flyer. It all began with a fear of flying that was so deep that the golfer decided that the only way to conquer it was to embrace it with all his might. He completed nearly 20,000 hours of flight time in various aircraft and obtained his pilot certificate. In 2011, he flew from Palm Springs to Orlando in his Cessna Citation X. He thought it would be the last day he would ever pilot a plane, as his pilot's medical certificate was experiencing that day. However, despite the fact that he never renewed it, FAA records reveal that he was issued a new medical certificate that same year.
- Less than a week after Palmer passed away, both Ryder Cup teams celebrated him at Hazeltine National Golf Club in Chaska, Minnesota. Players gathered to watch a video tribute and played tribute to this golfing legend by wearing a special logo, button, and pin. Palmer's bag from the 1975

Ryder Cup was also placed on the first tee as a tribute.

- In 2017, a Golden Palm Star on the Palm Spring Walk of Stars was dedicated to Palmer.
- In 2020, a commemorative stamp was issued by the US Postal Service to honor him.

IT'S YOUR TURN TO MOTIVATE SOMEONE ELSE!

Many people mistakenly think that golf is for the very wealthy, or that you can't master this game unless you start in your childhood or teens.

You have read the life stories of so many golfing legends who have started out with nothing—and have let their passion guide them to authentic greatness.

Simply by sharing your honest opinion of this book and highlighting the outlook and mentality of golfing greats, you can help others discover that golf truly is for everyone.

Thank you so much for your support.
I wish you the very best of success in
your experiences on the greens.

Scan the QR code for a quick review!

CONCLUSION

The next time someone tells you that golf is boring, we hope you help shed light on the error of their ways with some of the stories contained in this book. If you play golf yourself, then you know all about the sense of camaraderie you develop with players, caddies, and people from a host of golf-related industries you bump into on the green or at the clubhouse. This bond is often based on a mutual appreciation of nature—as a player, you know that the fairways and greens are far from static, inanimate features, carefully manicured for visual aesthetics. They can be a battleground as well as an oasis, a setting in which you encounter seasonal changes up-close and (if you're lucky) interact with wild animals and creatures.

The golf course is also one of the toughest mental and physical challenges you will encounter—a place where water hazards, trees, sandpits, and slopes and curves test the strength of your swing and your technique. And there is no one tried-and-tested method when it comes to golf. It is arguably one of the most creative sports there is in this respect, since some players prefer straight swings and others like to play with the curved flight of the ball.

Golf matches are long and involve several hours in the Great Outdoors. They require nerves of steel, patience, and keeping your eye on the prize. As these stories have shown, some of the world's greatest players have experienced anxiety and panic on play day. Recall José María Olazábal literally quaking in his boots during the Miracle at Medinah.

Golf is, in many ways, a game that symbolizes life. There is no way to evade seemingly insurmountable challenges. Things could be going your way and suddenly, one bad swing could result in a missed chance for a birdie or eagle —one you desperately needed to win. However, golfing greats know how to forge ahead and transform self-doubt into determination and resilience. Remember Jack Nicklaus, who won the 1986 Masters after being called washed-up by the press? Or Seve Ballesteros, who turned his bitter rivalry with Azinger into fuel for Europe's victory at the Ryder Cup?

Then there is the rivalry you encounter with other players. You certainly don't need to be Nick Faldo or Paul Azinger to want to beat someone in a game—so desperately you may be tempted into rattling them by refusing to let them change a ball. Some feuds that start at a golf club last a lifetime. Think Paul Azinger and Nick Faldo, who seemingly reconciled years after their battles on the greens, only to reveal a dislike that simply wouldn't budge.

Countering these rivalries are stories of friendship and mentorship. Think of the profound effect that Charlie Sifford had on players of color who came after him, or the gentle way that Seve Ballesteros restored Olazábal's self-confidence as they fought to obtain one of the world's most coveted trophies.

Or what about the unexpected friendship that arose between Francis Ouimet and his caddie, Eddie Lowery? You will recall that Eddie was just a little boy who played hooky from school and managed to walk alongside the man that would take home the U.S. Open in 1913 and become the first non-Briton elected Captain of the Royal and Ancient Golf Club of St Andrews. Eddie was just 10 years old when he became part of history! For a taste of what that match signified, take a look at the 1913 photograph of Eddie, standing in front of the crows with a towel around his neck, confidently gazing into the camera while the crowd lifted a jubilant Francis Ouimet on their shoulders.

For some players in these stories, life's biggest challenges have taken place off the course. Players who struggled against seemingly insurmountable obstacles included Lee

Trevino (who was lifted off the ground by lightning), or Ben Hogan (who, despite breaking his pelvis, rib, collarbone, and left ankle in a devastating car accident, won the Masters just one year later). Or what about Dennis Walters, who refused to let a golf cart accident (which left him paralyzed from the waist down) stop him from playing golf?

Then there are the wonderful rogues—the colorful, quirky characters who make great topics of conversation. Players like John "Monty" Montague, who was famed for his seemingly superhuman strength. Just the thought of Monty rubbing shoulders with some of Hollywood's biggest stars—from Bing Crosby to Johnny Weissmuller—is indicative of the power of golf to bring people together from all walks of life.

Some of golf's greatest achievers weren't rogues at all, if not highly gifted athletes like Tiger Woods (who many would say is one of the sport's GOATs) or Babe Didrikson Zaharias—a woman who defeated her opponents regardless of the sport she chose. Babe wanted to be the greatest female athlete who ever lived and many would say she wasn't far off her aim when she passed away at a young age from cancer.

And what about those wonderful rags-to-riches tales? Like that of Chi Chi Rodríguez, who dreamed of his next bite of food with every swing of his clubs? Or Ian Poulter, who may not have faced economic problems as sizeable as

Chi Chi's, but who had to prove his mettle for many years, working in a golf store until he caught the eye of a mentor who would change his life?

Golf is, in many ways, a tale of nobility. One in which, despite bitter rivalries, players acknowledge the unique position they are in to make a true difference on and off the field. Take Pia Nilsson and Lynn Mariott, who have dedicated their lives to motivating players, paying as much attention to the mental side of golf as to the technical one. Or Andrew Palmer, who spent much of his life on charitable work. Then there is Tiger Woods, who despite steering clear of polemic subjects, was not shy about the struggles he encountered earlier in his life as a black player.

Of course, if you asked the average pro player what is the best thing about golf, they would probably answer, "The friendships you make." Without a doubt, Jack Nicklaus won a buddy for life during his admirable concession at the 1969 Ryder Cup. Not to mention the beautiful friendships that centered around the great Seve Ballesteros. The Miracle at Medinah no doubt showed that some friendships last beyond life. Few doubted that on the day Europe took home the trophy, Seve was watching over them!

So if you've never visited a golf course before or taken that memorable first swing, what are you waiting for? This game will get your heart racing, do wonders for your mental health, and open your world to players from all walks of life. Above all, it will help you discover who you are, boost your confidence, and make you a far more resilient person than you ever thought you could be. It is perhaps fitting to end with sports psychologist, Dr. Bob Rotella, who once said, "Golf is about how well you accept, respond to, and score with your misses more than it is a game of your perfect shots." So pack up your clubs, head to your nearest golf course, and remember that you are playing a game that is a powerful symbol of how you stand up to the challenges that life throws your way!

REFERENCES

American Oceans. "Are Bull Sharks Dangerous?" Accessed October 4, 2010. https://www.americanoceans.org/facts/are-bull-sharks-dangerous/

Andalucia Golf. "Roberto De Vicenzo, the Greatest Winner of All Times." Accessed October 4, 2023. https://andaluciagolf.com/en/news/features/3203-roberto-de-vizenzo-the-greatest-winner-of-all-times

AZ Golf Homes. "Vision 54 Ranked One of the Top Golf Schools in the Country." Accessed October 1, 2023. https://azgolfhomes.com/vision54-ranked-one-top-golf-schools-country/

Bantock, Jack. "The 10 Most Bizarre Golf Courses in the World." CNN. December 16, 2022. https://edition.cnn.com/2022/12/16/golf/worlds-most-bizarre-golf-courses-spc-intl/index.html

Bantock, Jack. "The Butterfly Effect: How the Birth of Another Golfer's Child Led John Daly to an Astonishing Victory at 1991 PGA Championship." CNN. May 17, 2023. https://edition.cnn.com/2023/05/17/golf/john-daly-pga-championship-win-1991-spt-intl/index.html

Barton, John. "The Problem With Hogan." Golf Digest. May 24, 2019. https://www.golfdigest.com/story/the-problem-with-hogan

Bisset, Fergus. "1977 Masters: Watson Vs Nicklaus, A Taste Of Things To Come." *Golf Monthly*. June 30, 2023. https://www.golfmonthly.com/features/1977-masters-watson-vs-nicklaus-a-taste-of-things-to-come

Bisset, Fergus. "Ben Hogan Golf's Greatest Comeback." *Golf Monthly*. July 10, 2023. https://www.golfmonthly.com/features/the-game/ben-hogan-golfs-greatest-comeback-85672

Blumenthal, Steve. "On My Radar: An Infinitely Complex & Interconnected Global Financial System." CMG Wealth. July 17, 2020. https://www.cmgwealth.com/ri/on-my-radar-an-infinitely-complex-interconnected-global-financial-system/

Bobby Jones. "Bobby Jones the Legend." Accessed August 28, 2023. https://bobbyjones.com/pages/the-legend

Bonesteel, Matt. "Ben Hogan, Golf's Original Comeback Story, Roared Back from His Devastating Car Crash." The Washington Post. https://www.washingtonpost.com/sports/2021/02/24/ben-hogan-accident-tiger-woods/

Boswell, Thomas. "The Ryder Cup, a Tarnished Finish." The Washington Post. September 28, 1999. https://www.washingtonpost.com/wp-srv/WPcap/1999-09/28/005r-092899-idx.html

Boyette, John. "Jack Nicklaus, Others Look Back at 1986 Masters Victory." Augusta. https://augusta.com/masters/story/masters/jack-nicklaus-others-look-back-1986-masters-victory

Chiari, Mike. "Florida Golfer Fights Off Alligator with Putter." Bleacher Report. February 10, 2017. https://bleacherreport.com/articles/2692365-florida-golfer-fights-off-alligator-with-putter

Clearview Golf Club. "Renee Powell." Accessed September 30, 2023.https://www.clearviewgolfclub.com/reneepowell

Dixon, Troy. "Why Is Golf an Elitist Sport?" LinkedIn. July 11, 2017. https://www.linkedin.com/pulse/why-golf-elitist-sport-troy-dixon/

Donegan, Lawrence. "Faldo and Azinger at Pains to End the Bad Blood." The Guardian. September 17, 2008. https://www.theguardian.com/sport/2008/sep/17/rydercup.golf1

EDGA Golf. "Dennis Walters." Accessed October 2, 2023. https://www.edgagolf.com/profiles/15-dennis_walters/

Evans, Farrell. "Who Invented Golf?" History. June 20, 2023. https://www.history.com/news/who-invented-golf-origins

Fitzpatrick, Michael. "Is Bobby Jones' 1930 Grand Slam Season Overrated?" Bleacher Report. July 24, 2015. https://bleacherreport.com/articles/2530632-is-bobby-jones-1930-grand-slam-season-overrated

Golf Digest. "Tiger Woods Mourns Charlie Sifford While Seeking Answers to His Game." February 4, 2015. https://www.golfdigest.com/story/tiger-woods-mourns-charlie-sif

Golf Educate. "Average Age of a Golfer." Accessed September 30, 2023. https://golfeducate.com/average-age-of-a-golfer/

Gregory, Nicole. "The Mental Health Benefits of Golf as You Age."

Forbes. April 13, 2023. https://www.forbes.com/health/healthy-aging/mental-health-benefits-of-golf-as-you-age/

Hardisty, Matt. "The Concession - September 20, 1969." Ryder Cup. September 21, 2018. https://www.rydercup.com/news-media/the-concession-september-20-1969#:

Harig, Bob. "At 86, Sifford Still Making a Difference." ESPN. February 18, 2009. https://www.espn.com/espn/blackhistory2009/columns/story?columnist=harig_bob&id=3915271

Harig, Bob. "Golf's Honor Code Limits 'Cheating' Incidents." ESPN. August 7, 2007. https://www.espn.com/espn/cheat/columns/story?columnist=harig_bob&id=2964423

Hawkins, John. "The Masters Has Long Surpassed the U.S. Open as Golf's Favorite Major. Here's Five Reasons Why." SI. March 28, 2023. https://www.si.com/golf/news/five-reasons-why-masters-long-surpassed-u-s-open-as-golf-favorite-major#:

Howell, Elizabeth. "50 Years Ago, an Apollo 14 Astronaut Played Golf on the Moon. Here's the Inside Story." Space. March 3, 2021. https://www.space.com/apollo-14-moon-landing-golf-shot-analysis

Immelman, Mark. "The Timeless Lessons We Can Learn from Ben Hogan's Legendary Quotes." June 12, 2020. Golf. https://golf.com/instruction/ben-hogan-quotes-lessons/

Joseph, Anthony. "Keep Calm and Play On! Golf Club's VERY British Wartime Rules Where Players Could Pick Up Shrapnel, Replay a Shot If an EXPLOSION Hit and Take Cover from the Blitz 'Without a Penalty'." Daily Mail. January 20, 2018. https://www.dailymail.co.uk/news/article-5228409/Golf-clubs-British-wartime-rules.html

Kauffman, Peter. "Catching Up With Chi Chi." SI. March 18, 2021. https://www.si.com/golf/news/feature-2021-03-18-catching-up-with-chi-chi

Kelley, Brent. "Why Chi Chi Rodriguez Is One of Golf's Most Famous Players." Live About. February 5, 2019. https://www.liveabout.com/chi-chi-rodriguez-1562704

Kingdom. "The Origins of Augusta National." Accessed September 10, 2023. https://kingdom.golf/the-origins-of-augusta-national/

Kulkarni, Amey. "'The Electricity Stopped My Heart': Lee Trevino Once Explained How He Survived a Lightning Strike." Essentially Sports.

December 21, 2021. https://www.essentiallysports.com/golf-news-the-electricity-stopped-my-heart-lee-trevino-once-explained-how-he-survived-a-lightning-strike/

Lewis, Almee. "Duel in the Sun: One of the Greatest Contests in History." CNN Sports. July 21, 2017. https://edition.cnn.com/2017/07/21/golf/jack-nicklaus-tom-watson-turnberry-1977-duel-in-the-sun/index.html

Links Magazine. "Tommy Aaron: I Was There—The Collapse at the 1968 Masters." Accessed October 3, 2023. https://linksmagazine.com/tommy-aaron-1968-masters/

Long, Trish. "Lee Trevino Struck by Lightning: 'Your Whole Life Flashes before You.'" El Paso Times. https://eu.elpasotimes.com/story/news/history/2022/07/15/lee-trevino-saw-lightning-before-strike-during-1975-golf-tournament/65373017007/

Louis, Katrina. "Charles Sifford, 'The Jackie Robinson of Golf,' to Be Honored with Centennial Celebration in 2022." Q City Metro. June 21, 2021. https://qcitymetro.com/2021/06/21/charles-sifford-the-jackie-robinson-of-golf-to-be-honored-with-centennial-celebration-in-2022/

Lynch, Mike. "Why Ben Hogan Was the Greatest Golfer of All Time." Bleacher Report. January 2, 2013. https://bleacherreport.com/articles/1465256-why-ben-hogan-was-the-greatest-golfer-of-all-time

May, Jeffrey. "Why Is the Masters Played in Augusta?" AS. May 30, 2023. https://en.as.com/other_sports/why-is-the-masters-played-in-augusta-n-2/

McDaniel, Peter. "The Dawn of Dominance: An Oral History of Tiger Woods' 1997 Masters Win." Golf Digest. March 31, 2022. https://www.golfdigest.com/story/the-dawn-of-dominance-oral-history-of-tiger-woods-97-win

Mell, Randall. "Pia Nilsson, Lynn Marriott Reach Rarefied Air in Pro Golf's Coaching Game." NBC Sports. August 26, 2020. https://www.nbcsports.com/golf/news/pia-nilsson-lynn-marriott-reach-rarefied-air-pro-golfs-coaching-game#:

Melton, Zephyr. "Where I Played: The Home of American Golf, Pinehurst No. 2." Golf. March 6, 2020. https://golf.com/travel/where-i-played-pinehurst-no-2-first-time/

Michals, Debra. "Mildred "Babe" Didrikson Zaharias." Womens History. 2015. https://www.womenshistory.org/education-resources/biogra phies/mildred-zaharias

Montville, Leigh. "Legend from Lakeside." Golf Digest. May 5, 2008. https://www.golfdigest.com/story/gw20080509montville

Morse, Ben. "Moe Norman: The 'Rain Man of Golf' Who Amazed Even the Greats of the Sport." CNN. April 6, 2021. https://edition.cnn. com/2021/04/06/golf/moe-norman-golf-ball-striking-cmd-spc-spt-intl/index.html#:

Mosier, B. "Brookline, 1913: The Story of Francis Ouimet's Caddie, Eddie Lowery." NCB Sports. June 6, 2013. https://www.nbcsports. com/golf/news/who-was-eddie-lowery-francis-ouimet-1913-us-open-victory

Myers, Alex. "Did You Know: Golf Was Once Banned by a King." Golf Digest. Accessed September 30, 2023. https://www.golfdigest.com/ story/did-you-know-golf-was-once-banned-by-a-king

National Golf Foundation. "Golf's Biggest Participation Jump." Accessed September 30, 2023. https://www.ngf.org/golfs-biggest-participa tion-jump/

Nelson, Elizabeth. "Revisiting Jack Nicklaus's 1986 Masters Win, Through the Eyes of Those He Beat." The Ringer. https://www. theringer.com/2021/4/6/22368585/jack-nicklaus-1986-masters-win-nick-price-sandy-lyle-greg-norman-tom-watson

Owen, David. "The Story of Moe Norman, Golf's Troubled Genius." Golf Digest. April 1, 2020. https://www.golfdigest.com/story/the-story-of-moe-norman-golfs-troubled-genius

Park, Ryan. "50 Best Golf Quotes of All-Time." Avid Golfer. June 19, 2023. https://coloradoavidgolfer.com/50-best-golf-quotes-of-all-time/

Penn Live. "'Unmistakable' Golfer Payne Stewart Died in Airplane Crash 20 Years Ago." October 25, 2019. https://www.pennlive.com/sports/ 2019/10/unmistakable-golfer-payne-stewart-died-in-airplane-crash-20-years-ago.html

PGA Tour Media Guide. "Ian Poulter." Accessed October 5, 2023. https://www.pgatourmediaguide.com/player/bio/24138#:

PGA. "Lee's Enduring Passion for Coaching: 'I Love Watching Lights

Switch On'." Jun 4, 2022. https://www.pga.info/news/lee-s-endur
ing-passion-for-coaching-i-love-watching-lights-switch-on/

Piastowski, Nick. "Lee Trevino Was Asked Why He Keeps Playing Every
Day. Then He Got Emotional." Golf. December 17, 2022. https://golf.
com/news/lee-trevino-why-playing-emotional/

Planet Sport. "Ian Poulter." Accessed October 5, 2023. https://www.plan
etsport.com/golf/ian-poulter

Porter, Kyle. "How a Former Cowboys Player Helped Stop John Daly
from Committing Suicide." CBS Sports. November 2, 2016. https://
www.cbssports.com/golf/news/how-a-former-cowboys-player-
helped-stop-john-daly-from-committing-suicide/

Riess, Rebekah, and Zoe Sottile. "79-Year-Old Hospitalized After
Alligator Attack at Florida Golf Community." CNN. July 14, 2023.
https://edition.cnn.com/2023/07/14/us/alligator-attack-naples-flor
ida-trnd/index.html

Riverside Golf Bend. "Golf Demographics: How Many People Play Golf
and Who Plays It?" Accessed September 30, 2023. https://riversedge
golfbend.com/bend-oregon-golf-blog/demographics-of-golf/

Rooth, Ben. "Tiger Talk: The Best Quotes from Tiger Woods." Plant
Sport. Accessed August 20, 2023. https://www.planetsport.com/
soccer/feature/tiger-talk-best-quotes-from-tiger-woods

Rosaforte, Tim. "A Smash Hit: Dennis Walters, A Paraplegic, Inspires
Hope With a Nifty Trick-Shot Show." Vault. February 27, 1995.
https://vault.si.com/vault/1995/02/27/a-smash-hit-dennis-walters-
a-paraplegic-inspires-hope-with-a-nifty-trick-shot-show

Rothman, Evan. "These 16 Statistics Prove That Women's Golf Is on a
Serious Upswing." Golf. May 30, 2022. https://golf.com/news/
features/16-statistics-prove-womens-golf-upswing/

RTL Today. "Five Ryder Cup Controversies." September 27, 2023.
https://today.rtl.lu/sport/international/a/2118654.html

Ryan, Fergus. "Female Interest in Golf Continues to Rise Post-Covid."
Financial Times. July 15, 2023. https://www.ft.com/content/
b3fb6668-f603-4a3d-835d-1c814c4edcb5

Ryder Cup. "How It Works." Accessed September 1, 2023. https://www.
rydercup.com/what-is-the-rydercup

Schudel, Matt. "Charlie Sifford, Strong-Willed Golfer Who Broke Down

Racial Barriers, Dies at 92." The Washington Post. https://www.wash
   ingtonpost.com/sports/charlie-sifford-strong-willed-golfer-who-
   broke-down-racial-barriers-dies-at-92/2015/02/04/4a476aac-ac7e-
   11e4-9c91-e9d2f9fde644_story.html

Schupak, Adam. "Golf's most beloved figure, Arnold Palmer, dies at 87."
   Golfweek. September 25, 2016. Golfweek. https://golfweek.usatoday.
   com/2016/09/25/arnold-palmer-passes-away-at-87/

Schwartz, Larry. "Didrikson Was a Woman Ahead of Her Time." ESPN.
   Accessed September 20, 2023. https://www.espn.com/sportscen
   tury/features/00014147.html

Seve Ballesteros. "Remembering Seve." Accessed September 10, 2023.
   https://seveballesteros.com/en/remembering-seve/

Shipnuck, Alan. "The Greatest U.S. Open Ever." Vault. June 9, 2014.
   https://vault.si.com/vault/2014/06/09/the-greatest-us-open-ever

Sky Sports. "Ryder Cup 2012: Europe's Miracle at Medinah inspired by
   Seve and Ian Poulter." April 19, 2020. https://www.skysports.com/
   golf/news/12040/11975592/ryder-cup-2012-europes-miracle-at-
   medinah-inspired-by-seve-and-ian-poulter

Smith, Kyle. "Pinehurst No. 2 - An Amazing Golf Course." The Sporting
   Blog. Accessed September 12, 2023. https://thesporting.blog/blog/
   pinehurst-no2-an-amazing-golf-course

Southern Tide. "Why Has Golf Become So Popular?" Accessed
   September 30, 2023. https://southerntide.com/blogs/the-southern-
   edit/why-has-golf-become-so-popular

Stinson, Thomas. "The Master." The Atlanta Journal Constitution. April
   1, 2016. https://specials.myajc.com/jack-nicklaus-the-master/

The Richmond Golf Club. "Our Famous War Time Rules." Accessed
   September 30, 2023. https://www.therichmondgolfclub.
   com/Page/Custom?pageId=9096

Today's Golfer. "Why Ian Poulter Holes Putts When It Matters." July 8,
   2013. https://www.todays-golfer.com/tips-and-tuition/putting2/
   video-tips/2012/october/why-ian-poulter-holes-putts-when-it-
   matters/

Tom Watson. "About Tom Watson." Accessed September 30, 2023.
   https://tomwatson.com/about-tom/

Top End Sports. "Ben Hogan: Golf." Accessed September 30, 2023.

https://www.topendsports.com/athletes/golf/hogan-ben.htm#:

Tosches, Rich. "Breaking Silence: Two Decades Later, Goalby Finally Talks About De Vicenzo, 'Clerical Errors' and the '68 Masters." Los Angeles Times. April 12, 1989. https://www.latimes.com/archives/la-xpm-1989-04-02-sp-1531-story.html

UK Parliament. "The Reign of James II." Accessed September 30, 2023. https://www.parliament.uk/about/living-heritage/evolutionofparliament/parliamentaryauthority/revolution/overview/reignofjames/#:

Williamson, Oscar Johnson and Nancy P. Williamson. "Whatta-Gal" : The Babe Didrikson Story. London: Little Brown, 1977.

Made in the USA
Coppell, TX
02 December 2024

41614294R00111